Cracking the Code To Leadership:
The PAR Skills

G. Thomas Herrington

Patrick T. Malone

James Georges

ISBN 0-7414-4368-6

Edited by Diane N. Bates, Bates Communications

Cover design by John Clavijo, New Diameter Creative Services, Inc.

Published by:

INFI(∞)ITY
PUBLISHING.COM

1094 New DeHaven Street, Suite 100
West Conshohocken, PA 19428-2713
Info@buybooksontheweb.com
www.buybooksontheweb.com
Toll-free (877) BUY BOOK
Local Phone (610) 941-9999
Fax (610) 941-9959

Printed in the United States of America

Printed on Recycled Paper

Published June 2008

Table of Contents

Introduction

On a cold winter day in 1953, two Cambridge researchers, Dr. James Watson and Francis Crick, solved a mystery that literally changed the way people viewed human life. On that historic day, the two men cracked the elusive DNA code, discovering how a double helix in DNA carries life's hereditary information.

With their breakthrough, Watson and Crick not only uncovered the secret of life, but they also accomplished a feat other scientists had been attempting to do and had been writing about for years.

Another mystery that researchers, experts, and so many others have attempted to crack is the seemingly enigmatic secret behind leadership. Evidence of the hunt for the great leadership secret can be found in any bookstore, library, or online bookseller. Just look at the thousands and thousands of books written by authors and experts expounding on their theories on leadership or giving advice on the subject.

Among all those books though, you rarely will find any two with the same concept or theory. Every leadership book or manual seems to take a different approach. Some outline the habits of effective leaders; others analyze the various strategies behind leadership; and a seemingly endless list discusses the qualities, principles, laws, theories, and characteristics that successful leaders need.

In fact, quite a number of these books are by renowned government leaders and business icons, such as Winston Churchill, Colin Powell, Rudolph Giuliani, Lee Iacocca, and Jack Welch, who write about their leadership styles or recount their performances in crisis situations.

But despite this endless collection of leadership materials, finding a book that explains how YOU can be a better leader at work, at home, and in your community is virtually impossible. Instead, all these leadership authors and experts have concentrated only on the WHAT and WHY of leadership.

As a result, they never solved the leadership mystery because the secret is not in WHAT and WHY. The secret lies in HOW: *How to inspire others to wholeheartedly commit to a common course of action.*

After years of research and study, The PAR Group cracked open the mystery of leadership to reveal the skills needed to be an effective leader. In *Cracking the Code*, we share those leadership skills that will put you in control of your destiny: skills that make your goals realistic rather than just dreams; skills that build and nurture relationships; and skills that lead you down the path to success.

Cracking the Code is based on decades of research. Our studies started in the 1970s with our observations of countless people successfully leading others in the military and in businesses, teams, meetings, and organizations. We became intrigued by how some leaders were more effective than others at influencing followers, and we began to closely study leaders and their skills.

Using these detailed observations, along with the leadership experiences of our entire PAR team, we expanded our quest to understand the secrets behind leadership. We researched the psychology and behavior of leaders as well as observed people lead in both the business world and in everyday environments. And, of course, we read hundreds of leadership books and training manuals.

As a result of all this research, we made a discovery that is changing the way people view leadership. Leadership is not a mysterious process. Leadership, in fact, is just an intuitive, natural process of skills.

Think of all those instances when you were most successful in persuading other people to commit to your point of view. You got what you needed because others reached a level of confidence with your idea and acted on it. In other words, you led and people willingly followed.

When people succeed as leaders, no matter what the circumstances of their leadership roles, they exhibit a pattern of clear and definable skills. And, most importantly, that same set of intuitive leadership skills is used every time and forms the core of leadership and teamwork ability.

At PAR, we identified these skills and developed a comprehensive leadership and teamwork training application, so we could share our discoveries with others. And share we have.

Almost half a million men and women on six continents have learned the secrets of leadership and teamwork skills through PAR training applications. We have even tailored our training applications to specific work situations relating to selling, negotiating, coaching, supervising, customer service, management, self-directed work teams, or other business situations.

Yet, even though our PAR applications have met with worldwide success, we wanted still more people to have the opportunity to tap into their leadership skills, so we wrote *Cracking the Code.*

Covering the basics of our PAR leadership/teamwork training applications, *Cracking the Code* shows the skill set successful leaders use and, more importantly, shows **YOU** how to make those skills part of **YOUR** everyday life. To help you understand how the skill set works, we break leadership into interdependent, manageable chunks that are easy to see and do.

Each chapter explores a different element of the skills leaders use and gives examples of everyday business and personal life experiences. We also include easy-to-understand follow-up exercises to help you hone your own skills so that you can ultimately accomplish more at work, at home, and in your community.

The book, divided into five sections, follows our PAR Leadership Skills Model. The first four sections cover the essence of the PAR model, while the fifth offers real-life examples of PAR leadership at work.

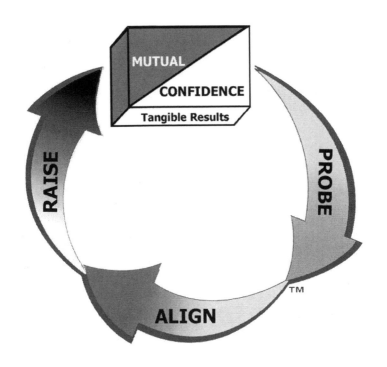

MUTUAL
CONFIDENCE
Tangible Results

RAISE

PROBE

ALIGN

™

PAR LEADERSHIP SKILLS MODEL

At the very center of the PAR leadership skills model is confidence because, after all, who would follow a leader who is not confident? In order to inspire someone to action, leaders must first believe in that action. Leaders are confident and committed to reaching targets, results, or goals. If a leader is not committed to achieving a goal, how can he or she inspire someone else to commitment?

Leaders may recommend strategies or action plans, but, make no mistake: a leader's focus is on the result, the end game, the goal. Leaders inspire others to have that same sort of confidence and commitment, so that mutual confidence occurs.

Leaders need more than just confidence in order to lead. To gain followers, leaders must know where those followers stand and what their perceptions are. So, leaders **PROBE**: They diagnose other people's points of view by carefully *listening* to more than just spoken words and *hearing* willingness and emotions.

After all, no matter what a recommendation or suggestion may be, not everyone is going to see it the same way. Pressing the point or forcing a certain view is only going to reinforce another person's viewpoint and not change his/her perceptions. Instead of forcing their views on other people, leaders *listen* to and *hear* other people's various points of view.

Is it not true that when you know exactly how and why someone feels a certain way, you are in a much better position to work with that person and provide suggestions that make sense to him or her? Ultimately, if others know exactly how you feel about an idea, they are in a better position to make modifications that make sense to you and raise your confidence in their approach.

Leaders do this intuitively; they tailor an approach to fit others' points of view, instinctively knowing what to say and how to say it. This innate sense of timing that the most successful business people seem to possess is a skill we call **ALIGNING**.

Once aligned with his/her followers, a leader can then inspire or cause his/her followers to think, feel, and behave in concert. By inspiring confidence, a leader gains buy-in, acceptance, support, or following from others.

Leaders instinctively describe how they reached confidence. They **RAISE** themselves in such a way that others can easily follow. This skill, which we identify as Raising, is an innate ability, one you undoubtedly experience every time you have a successful leadership encounter or inspire someone to a given course of action.

PROBE-**A**LIGN-**R**AISE (PAR) is the natural set of skills leaders use intuitively. *Cracking the Code* explains how these skills work and then shows you how to use **P**ROBE-**A**LIGN-**R**AISE over and over again, so they become part of your personal style.

Regardless of your level within an organization or what your job function may be, **P**ROBE-**A**LIGN-**R**AISE marks the very essence of success. These skills separate the outstanding performers from the rest of the pack.

By mastering the PAR leadership skills, you create win-win situations. You win because you achieve your goals, and those around you win because you help them get where they want to go.

Cracking the Code demystifies leadership and proves that leadership is simply the ability to wholeheartedly inspire others to follow a given course of action. We cracked the code of leadership for you.

Now it is your turn to use our secrets to transform yourself. Whatever level of success you have achieved already, when you master **P**ROBE-**A**LIGN-**R**AISE, your success will grow exponentially.

Section One

Cornerstones of PAR

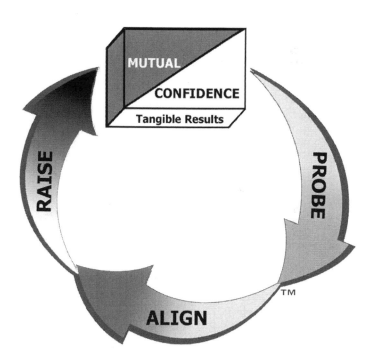

Chapter 1

The Decision Ladder

One of the golden rules of life you learned as a small child was to *stop, look, and listen.* Your parents told you to *stop, look, and listen* before you crossed the street, and when you were learning to drive, you were told to follow that same rule when you came to an intersection or railroad track.

Even today, whether you realize it or not, you *stop, look, and listen,* every time you pick up the remote and surf from one channel to another on your television. So, obviously, over time, you have mastered this golden rule, and it is now ingrained as part of your everyday life.

What you may not realize is that *stop, look, and listen* is an essential component to the secret of being a good leader. In fact, the leaders you see in business, politics, sports, education, and everyday life are those men and women who use this simple approach all the time.

Effective leaders STOP and pay attention to their potential followers. Leaders LOOK at the people they interface with, watching for emotion, checking to see if their audience, team, friends, co-workers, or employees are following or not...and looking to see whether they are angry, happy, excited, sad, cautious, or challenging.

Leaders also LISTEN. They listen to the music of communication – the tone, the speed, the inflection – always instinctively hearing more than just the spoken words and paying close attention to *how* people respond than to the actual words people use.

Take the simple statement, "I can't wait." Say these three words excitedly and with joy, and "I can't wait" takes on a sense of excitement and anticipation. Now say, "I can't wait," with sarcasm, and those words convey skepticism, hostility, or even anger. Even though you used the same three words both times, the meaning was entirely different each time.

So, you can see it is not WHAT you say but HOW you say it that is important. It is the emotion and its corresponding music of communication that color your words and effectively change their meaning.

Pets are perfect examples of listening not to the WHAT but to the HOW a statement is said. If you tell your dog, "I'm not going to feed you tonight," but you say it to him with a smile on your face and with a loving tone, your dog will wag his tail and look at you lovingly. He is listening to your tone and to the music of your communication, and not to the actual words you use.

People, too, have the innate ability to sense emotions. Even as a child, you instinctively knew if your parents were angry with you just by the tone of voice when they said your name. If your mother called, "It is time for dinner," you quickly realized, by the emotion in her voice, if you needed to hurry into the kitchen immediately or if you could stretch out another five minutes to watch television.

Behavioral scientists confirm the importance of emotions in communications, estimating that less than 10% of in-person communication is contained in the words that people use. This means that *over 90%* of the meaning of communication is in **HOW** words are spoken...in the voice and body language or the music of communication.

With face-to-face communications, you not only hear what is said, but you also see HOW the words are communicated, giving you a better interpretation of what is said. Telephone conversations are not nearly as effective because the visual expressions and body language that color communication are missing.

Email and instant messaging are less successful forms of communication because they almost completely eliminate the music of conversation. Some people try to color their messages by adding smiley faces, bold letters, or colored type, but these techniques are often misinterpreted and not consistently effective.

Consequently, even though face-to-face communication is the most expensive mode of communication, it is the most effective because you both see and hear the emotions associated with the words spoken.

Regrettably, the business world downplays the innate ability to read others' emotions. Instead, the focus in business is on processes and strategies, on what is logical and analytical, and on the head and not the heart.

Most business books and their expert authors boil these processes and strategies down into logical, rational sets of steps to follow – specific steps for coaching, managing, delivering feedback, and for teamwork, service, and even sales. While their leadership advice is sound, these business experts fail to include the HOW-TOs or directions on how to successfully implement these steps and, more importantly, how to stay effective even when a conversation or situation goes off script.

Analytical and logical listening is only part of reality. To be effective, you need more for leadership and success. You need to know the HOW-TO skills that we at The PAR Group have been training hundreds of thousands of people on for over 25 years.

Before we show you the HOW-TOs for influencing and for getting buy-in and commitment, we want you to first understand how people make decisions.

Herb Simon, the famed Carnegie Mellon professor and pioneer in artificial intelligence and cognitive psychology, spent years studying how decisions are made and won the Nobel Prize for his research in decision making. Captivated by how men and women actually make decisions, Simon conducted massive research, interviewing business people on their decision making. Over and over, he heard similar responses when he asked people how they came to decisions – "I feel better about this approach. It was a gut decision. My intuition just told me it was the right thing to do."

What Simon concluded in his theory of *Bounded Rationality* is that the human element plays a crucial role in decision making. In business, as in everyday life, men and women don't always make decisions based on logic alone. They make decisions that feel right at the time. In other words, people combine emotions with facts to shape their business opinions and decisions.

Unfortunately, most people are not accustomed to recognizing and labeling their own emotions from moment to moment, much less anyone else's emotions at any given time.

People ignore the world of feelings and mistakenly believe that the goal of leadership is to achieve intellectual agreement. The problem with this point of view is that effective leaders are looking for commitment, not just intellectual agreement.

Leadership would be easy if, when making decisions, people could depend entirely on facts. But they do not. How often do you have all the data that exists to make a perfectly rational, logical choice (especially in business decision making)? How often do you have an idea or suggestion all thought out in theory, but others do not see the information the same way? How many times, after all, do you think you have a commitment with someone only to find, when he or she does not act on it, that you only have a general agreement?

For you to gain followers and lead requires that people willingly commit to follow you, and as Professor Simon concluded, people do not decide anything based on logic alone.

Emotions *shape* the information coming to you and, consequently, affect decisions dramatically. This is important to know because if you are to lead and influence others to cooperate and share your convictions, you must focus on both the head AND the heart.

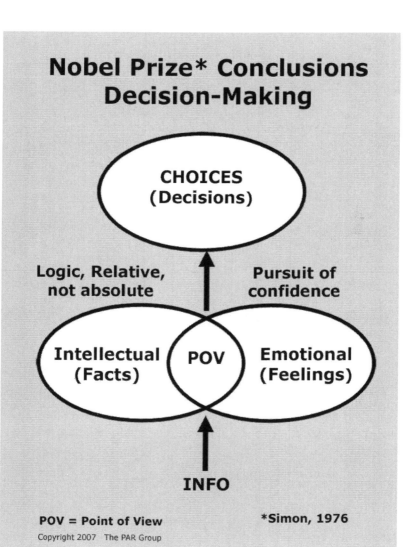

Since people overlay how they feel about the facts, decisions are often based on the course of action that is the most satisfying...what people are most comfortable with...and not necessarily the course of action that maximizes the cost-benefit ratios at the time. Not surprisingly, the bigger the decision, the more feelings or emotions come into play.

Take buying a home for example. A ConocoPhillips vice president in one of our training classes gave his own example of how emotion impacted a major decision he and his wife made. Since their children were grown and gone, he and his wife wanted to downsize and decided to look for a smaller home.

Even though they made a list filled with all their logical requirements for this smaller place, they ended up buying a farm with a larger house because they "loved" the view. For this couple, their hearts took precedence over logical facts and reasoning.

However, in business, people tend not to focus on emotions when it comes to decision making. The major reason for this is that most business experts fail to link logic to emotion and, instead, emphasize the need to concentrate on the principles and procedures engineered to facilitate intellectual agreement.

A few business experts, however, have recognized the emotional factor, referring to it as EQ or emotional intelligence. Yet, even though they have verified the importance of emotions, these EQ experts struggle with explaining HOW TO apply EQ in business conversations.

Unlike most specialists in business training, The PAR Group knows that facts and feelings, when experienced together, produce unique personal decisions, not computer logic. And we have developed the ability to coach that skill in others by creating practical applications for all business disciplines and job functions.

There is an old saying that is certainly true: *In order to lead, first you have to follow.* If you are to be an effective leader, you must first be an effective follower. You must be able to accurately read others and see things from their perspectives, at least initially. By empathizing with others, you are better able to determine how to make sense to others and how to lead.

Facts are relevant to emotion. For instance, if you have a friend who is afraid to go on a trip, no amount of logic or facts you give him about the benefits of the trip will make his fear go away. Instead, if you recognize his anxieties and listen to his fears, you are in a much better position to help him manage those fears and influence his attitude regarding the trip.

A person who is fearful about something perceives facts a lot differently than a person who is interested in that same thing. Effective leaders instinctively recognize this facts/emotion relationship and intuitively listen to emotions as well as to facts.

Over the years, business writers and experts have a hard time explaining this head-heart aspect of business. Because they see this as "touchy-feely" and uncomfortable, they constantly refer to leadership as an *art*. What we have done at The PAR Group is to demystify this *art of leadership* by creating a tangible, easily recognizable Decision Ladder that explains the intuitive *stop, look, and listen* ability often used in better leadership moments.

Using Professor Simon's Nobel Prize winning decision-making theory as our basis, we identified ten different points of view or emotional *attitudes* common to decision making. We simplified and organized these attitudes into a decision-making scale or ladder, and we ranked the ten attitudes...from complete negative indifference at the bottom...to neutral in the middle...all the way to positive confidence at the top.

The Decision Ladder

Degrees of In-the-Moment Motivation

	ACTIONS	ATTITUDES	MEANING
(+) Accepting	**COMMIT**	Confident	Sure. Of Course.
	PLAY	Enthused	Love it! Just imagine.
	CONTINUE	Interested	What about...? (Questions)
	STUDY	Reserved	Let me think about it.
Any Idea or Information (– Neutral)	**LOOK/ LISTEN**	Neutral	I'm open. We can discuss it.
Non Accepting (–)	**CHALLENGE**	Competitive	Yes, but... I doubt it.
	STOP	Hostile/Opposed	No, you're wrong. Forget it.
	AVOID	Fearful	I'm not sure. It is risky.
	COMPLAIN	Troubled	Too much of a problem.
	NEGLECT	Indifferent	Why bother. Not interested.

©1980-2007

As you see, on our PAR Decision Ladder, we coupled each of the ten attitudes with a corresponding action because attitudes are inside a person and, therefore, impossible to read. What you can see and read are the corresponding actions people take when they feel a certain way. For example, if your attitude towards your house plants is indifference, you will likely **NEGLECT** watering or feeding them. But if you are really interested in house plants, you will likely **CONTINUE** to learn about the care and feeding of each species.

As outlined on the Decision Ladder, **NEGLECT** is the action that someone with an indifferent attitude displays just as **CONTINUE** is the action that corresponds with someone with an interested attitude. So, as you study and incorporate the Decision Ladder in your leadership skill set, remember to better read the attitudes of your followers, focus on the ACTIONS you see.

One critical point you need to know is that when we describe an ACTION as negative, neutral, or positive, we are not implying that any one ACTION is bad or good, right or wrong. Each action is simply a clue to a person's level of involvement or engagement at any point in a discussion. Also, know that these attitudes are momentary and change as the discussion goes on. When new facts are introduced, people immediately determine how they feel about that information and often change their attitudes, moving up or down on the Decision Ladder.

Remember the decision-making model and Professor Simon's research. No one is always indifferent, hostile, or interested, even though it may seem that way sometimes, especially if you have a chronic complainer as a co-worker.

As evidence of this moment-to-moment emotional shift, ask the complainer what he really likes doing and then ask him to tell you why. We predict that you will likely see that complainer change his attitude and, in the blink of an eye, move up on the Decision Ladder from **COMPLAIN** to **PLAY**.

The PAR Decision Ladder organizes and simplifies what you have been learning your whole life about recognizing degrees of willingness, cooperation, motivation, or buy-in. To better understand this, think of the PAR ladder as a wind sock at the end of an airport runway. To reach your goals, you must pay attention, at all times, to which way the wind is blowing.

Just as the wind may change from moment to moment, so may your potential follower's attitudes change toward a given idea or course of action. These momentary ACTIONS are your wind sock for leadership. Being able to recognize and adapt is what enables leaders to influence other people.

For example, when you give someone directions to your home or office, you first ask, "Where are you?" to determine that person's location. Once you know where he is, then you can direct or guide him to you. This same principle holds true for a leadership discussion. As you engage in the skill of leadership, you must first be able to recognize WHERE your followers stand on the Decision Ladder. Knowing where the audience is at any given point in a conversation is a baseline skill of every effective leader.

In Chapter 2, we show you how to make this baseline skill part of your personal leadership skill set. First, we explain the Decision Ladder in further detail, breaking down each rung on the ladder and identifying typical words and phrases associated with each level. Then, we point out nonverbal clues that will help you correlate the ACTIONS you see with the appropriate ATTITUDES at any given moment in time.

Finally, we show you how the Decision Ladder serves as a strong foundation on which to build your skill of influencing others. With this skill, you will be able to succeed more often when a situation calls for leadership and teamwork to produce buy-in and commitment.

Being able to use the Decision Ladder is the first essential key to your cracking the leadership code and tapping into your own personal leadership skill. So, let's start to demystify leadership by turning emotion into something tangible you can recognize in your everyday conversations.

Chapter 2

Listening to the Music of the Conversation

Your boss assigned you the task of creating a plan to cut costs in your department. After spending days on the project, you are confident that the proposal you developed both cuts expenses and increases the company's bottom line. But, before you present your ideas to your executive management, you need your colleague's support.

The question is: How will your co-worker react when you ask for his buy-in? Will he be positive and accept your cost-cutting ideas? Will he be upset or maybe even hostile? Or will he be neutral and open to your plan?

The clues to his reaction will not be in the actual words he says, but in the HOW or the music of his communication...by his tone of voice, energy level, inflection, and facial expressions. In other words, you will be able to determine his attitude by his ACTION.

Here's where the PAR Decision Ladder comes in. Being able to identify a person's attitude by correlating it to an ACTION on the PAR Decision Ladder is the first secret to cracking the leadership code. Each of the ten levels on the ladder illustrate a degree of involvement in a given situation and each level 'up' the ladder indicates a person's increased willingness and involvement in a given idea or task.

To help you better understand the ACTION/attitude associated with each level, we created ten different responses that a co-worker might make to your proposal. After a brief explanation of the ACTION and attitude, we offer you a list of generic verbal expressions and nonverbal or music-of-communication clues. These clues will assist you in identifying the energy levels, inflections, and facial expressions that go with the attitudes and actions.

Our examples are divided into three basic categories, just like the Decision Ladder. At the bottom are the negative actions of **NEGLECT, COMPLAIN, AVOID, STOP,** and **CHALLENGE**; then neutral **LOOK/LISTEN** is in the middle; and on top are **STUDY, CONTINUE, PLAY,** and **COMMIT**. As you study the examples and the levels of ACTIONS and attitudes, remember all these reactions are perfectly normal and appropriate to the right circumstances where they lead to success. Pay close attention to the clues we give you as we start at the bottom of the ladder and work our way up.

"It doesn't really interest me. I don't have a stake in your department. My department's doing just fine."

ACTION = NEGLECT   Attitude = Indifference

When your co-worker says, "It doesn't really interest me," he is not necessarily telling you that he does not like your proposal or that your proposal is weak or without merit. He may simply not be interested in the issue, or he feels your idea is irrelevant to his area of interest. He is indifferent, and, therefore, his ACTION is to **NEGLECT** the information that you give him.

Further clues to his attitude lie in the music of how he says the words. If he gives you little or no eye contact, seems unresponsive, speaks slowly or in a monotone, or fails to give you complete attention, he is sending you a signal that he is definitely indifferent to your idea.

This co-worker's attitude and ACTION show that he is at **NEGLECT**/Indifference, the lowest level on the Decision Ladder.

To better identify people at this **NEGLECT**/Indifference level, look for one or more of these verbal and music-of-communication clues.

Verbal clues	**Musical clues**
"Not interested. Forget it."	Lack of interest
"It doesn't matter."	Low energy, dullness
"Ah, never mind."	Silent, uncommunicative
"No thanks, it's not important."	No or poor eye contact
"There's no point to it."	Unresponsive
"It wouldn't work here."	Pessimistic, fatalistic
"It's a dead issue."	Slow speech, monotone
"I give up. It's useless."	Not caring
Attending to something else	No reaction at all

In your everyday life, you encounter people with indifferent attitudes all the time. They are the people who did not vote in the last election because they were not interested. They are the ones who **NEGLECT** to return your voicemail message because your call is low on their priority list, or they do not care about why you called.

Everyone has been at **NEGLECT** sometime. With all the pressures of work and family, some things just are not high on the to-do list. The uncut yard, unwatered plants, and overflowing laundry hamper are all signs of **NEGLECT**. Other priorities took precedence over cutting the grass, watering the plants, and washing that load of clothes. **NEGLECT** at the office is no exception.

With all the demands, work loads, and schedules people have, some items fall to the bottom of the list, and some never rise to the top. Additionally, when people commit to certain directions in their personal or business lives, they sometimes become indifferent to other directions concerning the same subject.

"I can't help you! I need help with my own plan! Why come to me? I don't have time to do all the stuff I have to do!

ACTION = COMPLAIN   **Attitude = Troubled**

"I cannot help you...I do not have time to do all the stuff I have to do" is your signal that this co-worker views your request for his help as just another difficulty or troublesome problem he must face. He may even sigh, whine, and look pained or tired when he responds to you. Because he might be overwhelmed or stressed, you asking him to review a plan is a task that he sees as just one more problem he has to tackle.

People who react in this manner are at **COMPLAIN**/Troubled on the Decision Ladder. At this level, people perceive information as bothersome problems that represent struggle, effort, difficulty, hard work, or sorrow. Their whines and sighs could be viewed as cries for help.

Because of the whining nature of **COMPLAIN**, dealing with people at this level can be difficult. To help you easily identify people who are at **COMPLAIN**/Troubled, watch for the verbal and nonverbal (music) clues that signal **COMPLAIN**.

Verbal clues	Musical clues
"It's too hard."	Low energy
"This is a hassle."	Sighing, whining
"It's too late. It's too much. It's too (anything)."	Apologetic
"Things are bad now."	Looks pained or tired
"I can't. Why me...?"	Downcast eyes
"You always do this to me."	Slow movement
"You never...."	Sees only failures
"This is too much for me."	Slouched posture
"I will never get it all done."	Extreme exaggerations

How often do you hear people complain about the weather, traffic, fuel prices, or the state of the world? Everyone has been at **COMPLAIN** from time to time. Take the man, for example, who wins the one million dollar lottery and then **COMPLAINS** about the taxes he has to pay. Or the woman who receives a promotion but **COMPLAINS** about how many months she has to wait for it. Both these people are at **COMPLAIN** just as is the Democrat who gripes about the Republican's views on taxes or the Republican who whines about the Democrat's policy on military spending.

For most, **COMPLAIN** is a momentary level, but a few people have mastered the art of complaining, becoming classic whiners who never seem happy about anything.

The important fact to know about the **COMPLAIN**/Troubled level is that all people have periods in their lives when they are overwhelmed and overstressed, when the thought of one more project, one more assignment, or one more responsibility brings out a complaint or two.

ACTION = AVOID **Attitude = Fearful**

Fearful is the best adjective to describe this co-worker who believes he may risk his job by supporting your plan or even taking time to review it. When you approach him for his assistance, he may try to avoid the conversation, pretend to agree, or, in some cases, might even lie.

People who are fearful about ideas they view as risky, **AVOID** taking action. A person at **AVOID** may sometimes sound like a complainer, but his energy is more focused on **AVOIDING** any action so that he can evade the consequences he perceives as fearful or negative.

In decision making, when people view risks as outweighing rewards, they will **AVOID** making decisions. To pinpoint a person at the **AVOID**/Fearful level, look for the **AVOID** clues.

Verbal clues	Musical clues
"I'd rather not risk it."	Indecisive, unsure, hesitant
"I'd like to avoid that."	Stuttering ("I, I, I...")
"Gee, uh...I'm not sure."	Poor eye contact
"I'm afraid that..."	Short attention span
"Why me?"	Nervous, jumpy, fidgety
"Gee, I'm not a guinea pig."	Postpones, passes the buck
"I'm kind of worried that..."	Withdrawn, shy
"What if...?"	Imagines numerous risks
"I'll need to clear that with..."	Tries to change the subject
"I'd rather not take the chance."	Appeasement

While this attitude is referred to as fearful, this is not Stephen King, in-the-cemetery-at-midnight fear. This is the normal apprehension people routinely face when making significant decisions.

Remember the first time you presented a book report in front of your class or the first time you gave a presentation to a group of people? If you are like most people, you were apprehensive or uneasy and maybe even wanted to **AVOID** the presentation. After all, you were taking a risk doing something you had never done before. For instance, you may **AVOID** doing business with companies you see as credit risks. You may **AVOID** speaking against a pet project of a Senior Vice President because you fear that doing so could put your job at risk.

If you are a parent, how often have you **AVOIDED** making a decision by telling your child to ask your spouse for permission? Or have you ever not returned a voicemail to **AVOID** talking to a salesperson or not opened the door to that Girl Scout selling cookies?

You're out of your mind! That strategy is a big mistake. I won't have anything to do with it!

ACTION = STOP   Attitude = Hostile/Opposed

By saying, "I won't have anything to do with it," clearly this co-worker wants you to **STOP**...stop the conversation and stop the flow of information. He simply does not want to hear any more about your plan. He is opposed to your ideas.

People who respond in this hostile manner sometimes raise their voices, turn red, or become visibly angry. If they are opposed to a situation or idea they see as wrong, invalid, or unjust, they will remain opposed as long as the offending issue is part of the deal. In some cases, their extreme opposition may even turn into anger, but anger is less common in business than hostility.

Often in our PAR training classes, we have participants tell us that they think **STOP** should be at the bottom of the Decision Ladder because the ACTION of **STOP** is difficult for them to handle. Our answer, and what you need to keep in mind, is that the Decision Ladder is a measure of a potential follower's level of involvement. So, a person who is at **STOP** is much more involved with an idea than someone at any of the previous levels of **AVOID, COMPLAIN,** and **NEGLECT**. Some of the clues to use for determining whether a person is at **STOP**/Hostile include:

Verbal clues	Musical clues
"Cut that out."	Raises voice
"I don't want that."	Cold as ice, at times
"Wrong!"	Steady eye contact or staring
"I'm against that."	Ruthless, biting, sarcastic
"No. That way won't work."	Righteous (right/wrong)
"It's a bad idea."	Won't listen
"You are crazy."	Intolerant
"Stop it. Right now."	Blaming or threatening
"It won't work. It's wrong."	Demands control
"No way."	Swearing at times

Any time you stop a conversation, idea, or suggestion to prevent someone from going in a certain direction, you are at **STOP**. You are at **STOP** when you tell a fussy child, "I don't want to hear any more whining," when you tell the dog to **STOP** digging in the yard, or when you see the *No Smoking* sign. In business, you encountered **STOP** if you had an idea rejected, a vacation request turned down, or failed to receive a promotion you wanted.

An important fact to note is the close correlation between **STOP** and **AVOID**, the action that is one level below **STOP**. If a person at **AVOID** becomes intensely fearful, his reactions, if he is pushed, can quickly change from **AVOID** to **STOP**, as his anxiety level changes to hostility and opposition.

If I help you, what's in it for me? Who says your plan will do what you say?

ACTION = CHALLENGE   Attitude = Competitive

"Who says your plan will do what you say" is a **CHALLENGE** to your ideas. Your co-worker is not necessarily hostile or angry; he is just expressing his skepticism and doubts about your plan. Because he is **CHALLENGING** you, he argues and attempts to poke as many holes as he can into your plan.

He is at **CHALLENGE** on the Decision Ladder, and as such is someone who is competitive and places a high value on being right. His **CHALLENGING** action is designed to achieve a win, gain advantage, or change your mind.

CHALLENGERS often feel they need to change other people's minds through forceful persuasion, arguing about a proposed idea or solution and even attempting to find fault in it if they can. Those who **CHALLENGE** are saying, *show me,* because they need proof, justification, or rationale before proceeding. You can recognize **CHALLENGE/** Competitive by a number of verbal and action clues.

Verbal clues	Musical clues
"Are you kidding?"	Expresses doubt, skepticism
"Yes, but...I doubt it."	Contests, debates, argues
"Says who?"	Direct, forceful persuasion
"Prove it!"	Win/lose, Yes/but
"Come off it, will you?"	Upward voice inflections/ urging
"What for?" "Why not?"	Denies opposing views
That's too theoretical – it won't work in the real world.	High energy
	Aggressive
"How can you be so sure?"	Tests you
"I've heard that before."	Looks unbelieving

Go into any courtroom, and you'll see **CHALLENGE** at work as the prosecution faces the jury to prove that the defendant is guilty. In business, you find business executives using **CHALLENGE** as a time management tool. Usually inundated with hundreds of ideas, an executive's first reaction to a person with a new idea is to challenge that idea. When faced with such a challenge, most people take their ideas away for more work, thus freeing the executive from having to spend time right then on those ideas.

However, those few people who can handle the executive's challenge usually get his immediate attention. The lesson for you to learn here is that if you want your ideas to be viewed fairly, then you must be prepared to deal with challenge initially. Skepticism in the face of an idea is nothing new. Think of all the times you expressed doubts about an idea that seemed too good to be true or you needed more proof before you opened up to something new. **CHALLENGE** is a normal action and the most involved level on the negative side of the Decision Ladder.

I'll give you a few minutes. Tell me what you've got. Then I will decide.

ACTION = LOOK/LISTEN   Attitude = Neutral

When your co-worker says, "Tell me what you've got," he is open to your plan. In other words, he is neutral and willing to **LOOK/LISTEN**. At this point on the Decision Ladder, he is ready to **LISTEN** to options and alternatives and **LOOK** at the information you give him.

People with neutral attitudes neither reject nor accept ideas nor do they make any promises to act beyond this stage. At **LOOK/LISTEN**, conversation is polite and unhurried, and the atmosphere is usually relaxed. However, **LOOK/LISTEN** often is a fleeting position, with people either going up or down the Decision Ladder fairly quickly once they process the information they are given.

To determine if someone is at **LOOK/LISTEN** and has a neutral attitude, look for the verbal and musical clues.

Verbal clues	Musical clues
"I'll take a look."	Relaxed, no urgency
"No harm in listening."	Friendly, amicable, polite
"It might work. Who knows?"	Casual, leisurely pace
"No big deal."	Soft-spoken, pleasant
"I guess that's one possibility."	Laid-back, mellow
"That's cool. No problem."	Goes with the flow
"No complaints."	Not argumentative
"I'll hear what you have to say."	No commitments other than to routine matters
"I'm open."	Lacks vital interest
"Let's discuss it."	Interested, but not intense

People who read a newspaper, watch the nightly news, or go on the Internet for information are at **LOOK/LISTEN** on the Decision Ladder. Open to new data, they are neutral – neither for or against an issue.

A perfect example of **LOOK/LISTEN** occurs when you initially decide to consider buying a new car. From the moment you go to the classified ads or search on the Internet, you are at **LOOK/LISTEN**. While you read the ads and vehicle information, you remain open to all possibilities. But soon such factors as price, gas mileage, color, and accessories move you either up or down the Decision Ladder.

You drop down to **STOP,** as you eliminate some cars on your list. Or you transition up from neutral **LOOK/LISTEN** to **STUDY** because you need to analyze and review information about the cars that intrigued you.

I need some time to make my decision. Why don't you give me a copy of your plan for me to review.

ACTION = STUDY   **Attitude = Reserved**

When this co-worker says he wants to review your plan, he is indicating that he is not yet ready to commit but has made a decision to think about the plan. He is at **STUDY** on the Decision Ladder, wanting to analyze and review your information before making a final judgment. His attitude is reserved. Although your plan piques his attention, he is reserved and needs more time to research and reflect.

Unlike at **LOOK/LISTEN**, the level where people stay for just short periods of time, at the **STUDY** level, people take time to evaluate, analyze, think about, consider, and review the complexity of the decisions they must make.

You can identify a person at **STUDY**/Reserved by watching for the verbal and musical clues.

Verbal clues	Musical clues
"It's worth considering."	Fair, pleasant, positive
"Sounds realistic."	Slow to decide
"Reasonable..."	Reflective, analytical
"Well...I'll need more time."	Not overly friendly, but polite
"I need more information."	Conservative, mild interest
"Is there any research...?"	Weighs pros and cons
"I'll review it."	Good eye contact
"I'd like to sleep on it."	Suspicious of extremes
"Maybe we should get more input."	Satisfied with status quo

When you **STUDY**, you are on a quest for factual information. **STUDY** happens both at work and at home. You are at **STUDY** when you review the details of a proposal before accepting or rejecting it. You **STUDY** the sales contract before signing for your new car. And when you visit the CDC's Internet site to research the symptoms for the flu, you are **STUDYING.** In fact, this insatiable appetite to gather all the facts and **STUDY** information is the main reason that the popular Internet search engines are in business.

Exactly how much does your plan save your department? How long do you think it'll take before we see some results?

ACTION = CONTINUE   **Attitude = Interested**

When he asks, "How long do you think it'll take before we see results?" your co-worker shows he is obviously interested in your plan. He is engaged, attentive, and wants to **CONTINUE** the conversation. By being at **CONTINUE** on the Decision Ladder, he is indicating that he wants to explore, probe, and learn more about certain specific areas.

When a person is at **CONTINUE**, his attitude reflects interest, and he asks questions and is engaged. As the conversation **CONTINUES** and more questions are asked and answered, his need for additional information is satisfied.

When you recognize that your follower is at the **CONTINUE** level, be sure to answer all his questions before moving on. To determine if someone is at **CONTINUE,** look for specific verbal and action clues.

Verbal clues	Musical clues
"Tell me more...Sounds good."	High energy, involved
"How about...?"	Lots of questions
"Anything else?"	Good eye contact
"Good idea....Any others?"	Fast paced
"Interesting...go on."	Forgets about time
"Please continue. I like it."	Serious or smiling
"When could we start?"	Cooperative, constructive
"How would that work?"	Friendly, considerate
"Could you describe it?"	Full attention
"Nice idea. What else?"	Contributes, shares ideas

CONTINUE is focused. At this level, you are focused as you search for precise details. You need your questions answered on how a project is to be funded. You want to know not just if a car has a warranty but if that warranty specifically covers repairs on the brake rotors or the transmission. You need the specific names on the school board members, not just how many people are on the school board.

Finally, you will recognize a person as being at **CONTINUE**, because he or she is asking questions that are targeted, that show interest, and that **CONTINUE** the conversation with specific requests such as, *"What does it cost?"*

You know, your plan could work for my department, too. What if we tried this...

ACTION = PLAY   **Attitude = Enthused**

Now, this co-worker obviously likes your ideas. Saying "What if we tried this?" shows he thinks your plan has merit, and he is imagining how it will work. He is at **PLAY** on the Decision Ladder, a level where a person becomes engaged, has an enthused attitude, and **PLAYS** with an idea.

When at **PLAY**, a person has already decided that an idea might work, and he plays with that idea, visualizing how his goals will be met and imagining success and satisfaction.

To determine if a person is at **PLAY**, look for signs of his enthusiasm. He will show his enthusiasm by smiling, being cheerful, or maybe even joking. Also, use the verbal and musical clues associated with the enthusiastic person at the **PLAY** level.

Verbal clues	**Musical clues**
"Yeah. That's really good."	Happy, smiling, laughing
"I wonder if..."	Bright, wide eyes
"That's a terrific idea."	High energy
"You know...if we..."	Fast speech
"Let's play with that idea."	Eager
"Come on. Try it."	Physical motion, action
"I love it!"	Joking

In business, many people often mistake the enthusiasm that comes with **PLAY** as a commitment and then fail to understand why no follow-through happens. A perfect example of confusing **PLAY** for commitment comes from an American expatriate we taught in Germany. He emailed his co-workers saying, "Let's hold an American football game, and I'll teach you how to play." He was excited by the number of enthusiastic emails he got with people saying, "Let's think about bringing beer. Maybe we could have a picnic....Great idea...Sounds like fun."

Then at 10 o'clock on Saturday morning when the game was scheduled, no one came. Later, when the American re-read his emails, he realized that none of his messages said, "See you at 10!" While those he had invited to play American football were enthusiastic, they never committed to actually showing up.

The key to understanding the enthusiasm of **PLAY** is to think of **PLAY** as the highest level of good intentions at that moment in time. With **PLAY**, you play with an idea, imagining the results. Take buying a new big screen television, for example. If you are like most people, before you make the purchase, you **PLAY** with the idea of where to place the television in a room and how your favorite program would look on the big screen. As you enthusiastically **PLAY** with the idea of owning a new television, you move along the Decision Ladder.

No doubt about it. Your plan will work. Let's meet with the V.P. of Operations right away!

ACTION = COMMIT   **Attitude = Confidence**

When your co-worker says, "Your plan will work, and I support it," he not only likes your plan, but he is also committed to helping you. His attitude is one of confidence because he is fully decided and feels good about his decision. At the top of the Decision Ladder at **COMMIT**, he is now a co-owner of your cost-saving plan.

When people **COMMIT**, you have their complete buy-in, and they feel assured, positive, and calm about their decisions. Because they are confident in their commitment and are now co-owners of your idea, they will see the idea through to completion and help remove any obstacles that may occur along the way.

You can identify **COMMIT**, and easily distinguish it from **PLAY**, by looking for the verbal and musical clues that show confidence and commitment.

Verbal clues	Musical clues
"Yes, I am sure."	Calm, relaxed, positive
"Certainly."	Assured, committed, decided
"Absolutely."	Good eye contact
"No doubt about it."	High energy, full attention
"OK!"	Assertive, but kind
"Positively!"	Powerful
"I know it."	Convinced
"No question."	Downward voice inflections
"You can count on it!"	Strong, firm voice
"Exactly...I will...I expect..."	In complete self-control

COMMITMENT is making the decision. You **COMMIT** when you buy a car, a house, or that big screen television, and you **COMMIT** when you agree to accept a new job, sign a contract, or set a day and time for a luncheon meeting.

In business, **COMMITMENT** is you owning the company's objectives as much as your CEO does. At **COMMIT**, you become a co-owner of what you commit to, and your **COMMITMENT** becomes your sacred promise.

Summary

The PAR Decision Ladder with its ten different ACTIONS and attitudes is the cornerstone of personal leadership skills. Once you can correctly identify the ACTIONS, you are better able to understand people as they decide about cooperating or doing business with you. The Decision Ladder is a guide to help you understand other people better...not a tool to manipulate them.

We encourage you to practice using the Decision Ladder so that you become exceptionally good at recognizing momentary attitudes. Your goal should be to identify a person's ACTION/attitude within 10 seconds or less and with 90% accuracy. If you identify the ACTION within one level of where a person actually stands on the ladder, you can do business with that person. If you are off more than one level, your chances of effective communication with someone are virtually impossible.

You must also know yourself and your own decision-making ACTIONS as they happen. When you are able to recognize the clues for your own feelings, you can better identify the emotional clues of others.

If you are to be a successful leader, you must lead from the top of the Decision Ladder, from a level of **CONFIDENCE**. After all, the people you most admire are those who are confident, who take you seriously, who care about how you see things, and who want you to succeed.

Make the Decision Ladder part of your everyday life...use it at work, at home, at church, and at social get-togethers. Soon, you will see that ACTIONS speak louder than words as you pay more attention to HOW people say things rather than to what they say. And you will have taken that important first step to *cracking* the leadership code.

Chapter 3

Decision Goals

The other cornerstone of PAR is everyone is, in fact, a Decision Maker.

Keeping this in mind, start observing how leaders around you start their conversations. You should quickly notice that most leaders begin conversations differently than other people. Why? Because leaders know intuitively that everyone is a Decision Maker, regardless of a person's role...whether he is a subordinate, a team member, someone from another department, or even a superior.

Think about children cleaning their rooms. Some do it right away, while others need to be told ten times. Some do it right; others pile everything in their closets. How well do they follow what their parents say? They are all little deciders, aren't they?

Then, when the children become adults and go to work, some show up for meetings early, some show up just in time, others are always 15 minutes late, and still others just do not show up at all. Everyone is a Decision Maker, and each decision varies. Everyone decides just how much effort and willingness to put into each decision.

Have you ever thought about those first few seconds when you start to interact with another person? Or about just how important those initial moments are to setting the tone and the outcome of a business conversation or meeting?

Those first 15 seconds of any leadership interaction are critical because those initial seconds set you up for either success or failure. In this chapter, we will explain why those all important first seconds are significant, and then you can decide if using Decision Goals to initiate a leadership situation will help you be more successful.

In those first make-or-break seconds, the most effective leaders know their potential followers need leaders who:

Show they are **Confident** in the goals they advocate,

Invite Others to Neutral, as they explain the strategy for achieving the goals, and

Acknowledge others (their followers) as **Decision** Makers.

These three actions are the basic criteria for establishing specific Decision Goals for an interaction. We even started this chapter with a Decision Goal.

Go back a page and reread the sixth paragraph. Did you notice our statement of **Confidence**? The first 15 seconds of any leadership interaction are critical because those initial seconds set you up for either success or failure.

Then, did you find our **Invitation to Neutral** on the Decision Ladder? *We will explain why those all-important first 15 seconds....*

And finally, did you see how we acknowledged you, the reader, as the **Decision** Maker?...then you can decide if this chapter on Decision Goals will help you be more successful.

Clearly, in just two short sentences, we accomplished our goal of showing you our confidence, inviting you to a neutral point, and, most importantly, acknowledging your role as Decision Maker. After all, you are the Decision Maker in this case. You decided to buy this book. You decided whether or not to buy-in to the concept of the Decision Ladder in the first two chapters.

Now, you are at your next decision point, deciding whether or not to buy-in to Decision Goals as a more effective way to start your leadership interactions. But before you make that decision, we want you to better understand what is behind our Decision Goal concept.

First, answer this: How many times have you been in a business meeting where a great deal of discussion took place, loads of questions were asked, and yet, after a couple of hours, no productive decision occurred?

Or maybe the only decision reached was to continue the discussion at another meeting, which was destined to end with the same dismal results. Unfortunately, this happens all too often. Productivity experts believe that as much as one-third of a person's business day is spent in unproductive meetings.

This situation of un-productivity deteriorates even more in community organizations, nonprofit groups, or volunteer groups. Well-intentioned people debate for hours the *whichness of what,* while long, drawn-out meetings yield far fewer results than they are capable of ever producing.

Or, how about frustrated parents with an unruly child? How often have you watched a parent threaten a child for the fourth or fifth time, saying, "This is the last time I'm going to tell you to stop hitting your sister...or stop whining...stop picking up that candy...stop standing on the furniture"...and the list goes on.

Unfortunately, in today's complicated, busy world, most people just do not have enough hours in the day to accomplish everything needed to be done. Yet, people still attend business meetings that waste their time and community or volunteer groups that waste their talents. And, in too many cases, as with the frustrated parents, people invest time in meaningless threats that yield no behavioral changes and only add stress to their only safe haven – their families.

Obviously, there has to be a better way, and there is. The answer is in the three criteria for creating effective Decision Goals: **Confidence**, **Inviting to Neutral**, and **Decision**. These keep conversations and meetings focused and enable them to reach actionable conclusions.

1. Confidence

A leader cannot inspire anyone to a higher point of view than his own viewpoint. That is why it is absolutely essential you believe in the goal you advocate and why confidence is the first criteria of a good Decision Goal.

In the late 1980s, a little-known Atlanta businessman, Billy Payne, dreamed of bringing the Olympics to his hometown. Privately he worked with his dream until he had transformed it into his belief. Only then did he take his idea public where he was greeted by smiles, polite nods, and even derision behind his back. Unshaken, he believed in his idea, and he continued to spread his vision of what could be to the movers and shakers in Atlanta, in the United States, and ultimately around the world to the International Olympic Committee. Billy Payne's confidence was rewarded with the 1996 Summer Olympics. Without that confidence, he would have long ago abandoned his Olympic idea and returned to his business pursuits.

Bernie Marcus and Arthur Blank believed they could succeed in the home improvement business in spite of having been fired from a leading home improvement retailer. Their confidence gave birth to Home Depot. Sam Walton's confidence created Wal-Mart and made him a billionaire many times over. Bill Gates, Donald Trump, Jack Welch, Lee Iacocca...the list of recognized leaders and their confidence is endless.

But you want to know how this applies to you. You are not trying to stage the next Olympics or build a better Wal-Mart. All you really want is budget approval to buy the new software for your financial system. All you really want is your colleagues' help on the new database project. All you really want is the sales vice president's approval for an additional salesperson in your district.

The same confidence that delivered the 1996 Olympics to Atlanta and built Home Depot and Wal-Mart can deliver the software, cooperation, or additional person you want. By using the three "all you really want" examples mentioned before, we will show you how to demonstrate **Confidence**.

1. *Software* – I am <u>convinced</u> we can increase the speed and accuracy of our financial reporting system through the acquisition of a new software package.

2. *Cooperation* – I <u>believe</u> we can increase our customer service, decrease our current inventory levels by 10%, and grow our business by 15% by improving the quality of our current database.

3. *Salesperson* – I <u>can deliver</u> 100% return on investment of an additional sales territory in my district within the next 18 months.

As you can see, each statement opens with a strong statement of **Confidence.**

Before we go any further in talking about Decision Goals, we want to point out an important paradox of leadership, and that is the difference between goals and strategy. A goal is where you are going. Strategy is how you are going to get there. Unfortunately, many leadership initiatives fail because people become so locked on their strategies that they neglect to clearly articulate the goals.

In the first example we just gave, the goals are stated first – speed and accuracy of financial reporting, increase customer service, decrease inventory and grow revenue, and 100% return on investment. The strategies on how to achieve the goals come next – new software, improved database, and an additional sales territory.

Why state goals separately from strategy? First, and foremost, by keeping your goal and strategy separate, your followers are more inclined to buy-in to the potential value or benefits of your idea. Also, remember that as you state your goal, you should identify for your followers how they will benefit or what's in it for them.

The other reason goals and strategies should be separated has to do with another paradox of leadership. Leaders are simultaneously inflexible and flexible. They are absolutely inflexible when it comes to their goals, but they are extremely flexible regarding strategy.

A leader, presenting our three examples, could be flexible to alternatives to new software that could deliver more speed and accuracy. A leader could be open to other options for that improved database or additional sales territory. But a leader would not compromise on the goals.

When Jack Welch launched General Electric into its "first or second in your industry or you're sold" goal, he was absolutely inflexible. Yet, paradoxically, he showed he was incredibly flexible in how GE met that goal when he allowed each division to develop their own strategies for achieving his ultimate goal.

Again, using our examples, the vice president of sales is more likely to listen to your ideas if you lead with increased sales versus leading with adding a new sales territory. Your colleagues are much more likely to help with your database project if they think they can reduce inventory, increase revenues, and improve customer service. And, finally, that CIO or CFO will be much more inclined to listen about your new software proposal when you open your discussion with the phrase *increased speed and accuracy.*

Each of the examples we have given you prove an essential truth regarding leadership: True leaders help people get where they want to go, and in the process, leaders acquire followers for their own goals.

2. Invitation to Neutral

In an ideal world, every potential follower would enter a conversation totally committed to the leader's goal. But this is the real world where, during interactions, followers can take a variety of positions related to the leader's goal. Some people may be apprehensive while others will be interested. Some may be opposed and others enthusiastic. Some may want more proof while others require more time to study the idea.

Leaders realize that differing points of view are natural, and, because of that, they see opposition not as a negative but as a positive and a way to strengthen those ideas. However, the one thing every leader wants is the opportunity to get his idea out for discussion, and the most effective way to accomplish that is by expressing an explicit **Invitation to Neutral**.

How do you invite a person to neutral? Go back to the examples we used earlier when we discussed **Confidence**, and you will see that each example contains an *invitation* to the other person to a neutral, **LOOK/LISTEN** level:

1. *Software* – "Let me explain why I am advocating a new software package..."

2. *Cooperation* – "Let's discuss the database improvement project..."

3. *Salesperson* – "I'd like to show you my projections based on a new territory..."

Inviting people to neutral sends a powerful message to potential followers. By doing so, you are saying you are so confident in your goal that you are willing to invite others into a no holds barred, open discussion of pros and cons.

As you undoubtedly have realized, this going to neutral approach is quite different from how most people operate, especially a lot of salespeople.

How often have you encountered a salesperson only interested in selling his idea, product, or service? If you are like most people, you resisted that kind of approach. Unfortunately, what often happens is that when a salesperson sees resistance like yours, he sells even harder. The result is a descending spiral that usually leads to resentment and broken relationships.

While salespeople may be easy targets to relate to, this same *Buy this, Buy this* behavior is often exhibited by managers. Rather than open an idea for discussion, many managers use their positional or economic power to gain acceptance of their ideas. These managers end up with compliance, and, unfortunately, with a workforce that is not motivated and, more importantly, a workforce that takes no ownership of the company's, division's, or department's goal.

A much better approach is the explicit **Invitation to Neutral** which leads to a sincere and frank discussion of an idea. Bringing someone to neutral or **LOOK/LISTEN** is as critical a component in good decision goals as is **Confidence**.

3. For a Decision

No doubt you have been in business meetings that consumed countless hours and yet produced few results. You probably have been in community or volunteer meetings that wandered around aimlessly, wasting the collective talent of all those in attendance. And, more than likely, you have encountered mothers and fathers arguing with their children in public.

What is happening in each of these cases is that no one clearly has articulated up front what the intended outcome of the interaction should be. Put in the simplest terms, what is lacking here is a **Decision.**

Again, go back to the three examples we have been using and review the last portion of each one:

1. *Software* – "Then you can determine if the purchase of the new software is in our best interest."

2. *Cooperation* – "And then you can decide if you will be part of the database project team."

3. *Salesperson* – "Then, if it makes sense, you can support my request for an additional sales territory."

Look at the decisive words we used – *you decide, you determine, you support.* What we did here is acknowledge the other person as the Decision Maker. This is a simple process and perhaps the reason why Decision Goals are so powerful.

An effective leader looks for his followers to reach a willing and committed decision at the end of any leadership interaction. By acknowledging that other people have the power of deciding, a leader implies that he is just as okay with a willing and committed **YES** as he is with a willing and committed **NO.**

When you reach this same level of comfort, you will have tapped into one of the truly great sources of influencing power. However, being okay with a **YES** or a **NO** is not easy for some people. If your goal is to make a sale, get your project funded, add a sales territory, or buy the software, you start out from a position of weakness. Let us explain why that is.

When you first make your pitch for a product or idea, you do not know if you can make the sale. If you do, you win, but if you don't, you could lose. What you have created for yourself is a classic win-lose scenario. When faced with a possible loss, if you are like most people, your reaction will be to sell harder until you do something stupid like give the product away or destroy the potential relationship.

A better way is to create a win-win situation. You do this by letting go of the need for a **YES** answer and being open to either **YES** or **NO**. This immediately delivers a win-win for both you and your potential follower. After all, what the follower wants to do is to *make a decision*, and if you want to *get a decision*, then you must create a common goal for the conversation. You become the Decision Getter and your follower is the Decision Maker.

If you do get a **"NO,"** accepting it with good grace will allow you to come back later with a different approach to reach the goal. A **"NO"** is only a **"NO"** for now. But if you continue to push to get only **"YES,"** more often than not, you will get a **"NO"** forever and not be welcomed back. Which would you rather have: a **"NO"** for now or **"NO"** forever?

So often the initial decision being made is not a full **YES** or **NO** decision, but rather how much effort to expend or how willingly to take on the assignment or task. That willingness is in fact a decision and has a lot to do with the final outcome. Being in a position of authority will definitely get results, but not the results that full commitment and buy-in do.

Decision Goals will work for you whether you are in sales, customer service, supervision, management, or whether you are an individual contributor, part of a team, or an executive leading a major change initiative in your company.

In the next short paragraph, we use the three criteria as we wrap up this section on Decision Goals. Pay attention to how the **Confidence**, **Invite to Neutral**, and **Decision** are woven into our discussion:

> *"We are convinced that establishing Decision Goals within the first 15 seconds of any leadership interaction will help you be more successful. (**Confidence**) Let us share a number of examples with you (**Invite to Neutral**) and then you can decide if Decision Goals have a place in your business and personal life (**Decision**)."*

Examples of Decision Goals in Use

<u>CEO addressing the Board of Directors</u>

"I am convinced that we will continue our growth and protect our market position through an orderly succession process. Let me explain the succession plan in some depth, and then you can determine whether or not this proposal is in the best interest of the shareholders."

<u>CIO to potential project members</u>

"Our current database no longer efficiently serves the changing needs of our business model. Since each of your areas depends on the database, I have selected you as potential members of the database project management team. Let me review your respective roles and responsibilities, and then each of you can decide if you can commit to being part of this project team."

<u>Sales Vice President to Operations Vice President</u>

"We have a $20 million opportunity with our key customer if we can double pack our X-47 widgets. Let me show you what we need to have, and then you can determine if it's feasible to alter the process."

<u>Sales District Manager to Director of Sales</u>

"I can sign the university regents to a long-term contract if I can include a specialized application to meet their RFP requirements. Let me review the requirements, and then we can decide if the specialized application is feasible and then secondly if it is in our best interest."

<u>Individual Contributor to Project Leader</u>

"I believe we can improve our communications and reduce the number of reworks by conducting a monthly on-site visit with our primary suppliers. Let me review the proposed checklists for each visit as well as the estimated travel costs. Then you can decide if the savings will justify the added travel time and costs."

Meeting leader with a focused agenda

"I believe we have all the marketing information we need to determine if the X26 prototype should go into limited production. So, our mission today is to do a final review and then determine if it is a go or no-go."

Meeting leader recruiting participants for a brainstorming session

"Our customer service initiative is going no place. You guys are closest to the issue, and I believe if we get together for brainstorming sessions, our options will be clear. Let me explain why I want your participation and how the meeting will be conducted so that you can determine if you want to be included."

Supervisor providing corrective feedback to employee

"As you are well aware, we have a very clear dress code in this organization and the current attire is in violation. Let's review the policy so that you can decide whether or not you are able to comply."

Supervisor coaching session with average performing employee

"Your current level of performance is certainly meeting the basic standards for customer service, and that is commendable. My sense is that you definitely have the capacity to do even better and become part of the President's Club. I would like to share a few ideas I have and would be interested in hearing your ideas also. In the end, you can decide whether the extra effort is worth the rewards and recognition that go along with becoming a member of the club."

Salesperson prospecting for new business

"Our proprietary content and coaching methodology has helped many businesses similar to yours increase revenue and decrease expenses. I am not sure we can help your organization because I don't have an in-depth knowledge of your situation. So, a brief conversation about your needs and our capabilities would be the recommended next step. Then you can determine if a face-to-face meeting is appropriate."

<u>Community or nonprofit leader opening a meeting</u>

"I am convinced we can generate the funds to underwrite our programs by sponsoring a book festival. Let's discuss the pros and cons of this type of fund-raiser, and then we can decide if this is something we can all support."

<u>Dad working out a problem with his teenage daughter</u>

"I believe you can make good on your commitment to Mom and still go to the party on Friday evening. Let me share a couple of ideas that will resolve the scheduling conflict and then you can decide if they are workable."

To put this in action for yourself, structure your opening statement in the form of a Decision Goal:

Confident Statement: What is your idea, suggestion, or approach you believe in? What is the potential benefit or outcome that would be of interest to the person or audience you will be talking to?

Invitation to Neutral: Invite them to talk about it or listen to it.

Decision: So they can decide whatever decision you are seeking.

Now that you have the criteria and a number of examples of Decision Goals at work, we are confident you can use these to create real Decision Goals for you and your specific situations. Decision Goals work, as our clients will tell you.

Many times in our PAR training sessions, we hear salespeople complain about not being able to get appointments with the right Decision Makers. Assuming the salespeople have done their homework on their prospects, those same salespeople get results when they use Decision Goal criteria and our coaching to frame a prospect call that works. Usually, more than 50% are able to make appointments during the training session. Of the rest, another 50% obtain appointments within one week of the PAR session.

One of our clients, a Hewlett Packard executive, recounted how his professional service group bogged down in long, seemingly endless client meetings. After attending our PAR training, his team reduced their meeting time by as much as one-third and increased their actionable items by a similar amount. Starting their meetings with Decision Goals helped them compress the decision-making cycle.

Another PAR client, David Solberg, an executive for a major manufacturer, credits Decision Goals with helping boost his company's overall sales numbers. According to David, using Decision Goals enabled the company's sales personnel to get a fair hearing for their products.

We also had a client in Germany use Decision Goals in an entirely different way. Working in a highly structured environment, the Decision Goals gave the people there a way to present their ideas to their managers without usurping the managers' powers.

After working with over half a million people for almost three decades, we have quite a few success stories. But this is the time for you to write your success story. Adding Decision Goals to your intuitive leadership skills will dramatically improve your results. Try it and you will discover what so many already know. Decision Goals work.

Section Two

"P" for PROBING

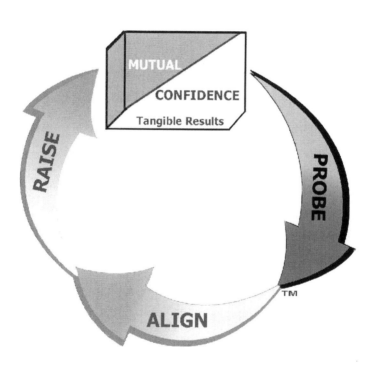

Chapter 4

Building Rapport

In order to lead, you first have to follow.

You already know how to recognize the degree of following on the Decision Ladder. However, just knowing where a person is on the Decision Ladder is not enough. You also have to be able to read the situation from that person's point of view.

To do that, you make it easy and safe for people to talk. You show respect for what they have to say, regardless of whether they are a teammate, employee, superior, family member, or friend. You LISTEN.

How many times have you had someone say, *"You are not listening to me! You obviously don't care!"* or accuse you of not listening or paying attention to what was being said?

Without effective listening, communication fails. Unfortunately, the failure to communicate happens all too often in business conversations and personal interactions. So, how can you prevent a communication failure, and how do you show other people that you hear what they are saying?

The answer is obvious and one that you probably have heard or read dozens of times: *Listen with empathy...listen with understanding.* Effective listening has been taught for ages. In fact, almost every leadership book, as well as hundreds of books on personal relationships, talks about the importance of listening with empathy.

Yet, how many people actually listen empathically, making that effort to show that they actually understand or hear what is being said? For example, do salespeople listen? What about your managers, your spouse, your teammates, your employees, or even your children? Are they good listeners? We bet that if you ask any one of them that question, the response you get probably will be, "I listen fine. Everyone else has a problem listening."

Unfortunately, too few people in today's world are good listeners. Most people fail as effective communicators because they let their ineffective listening habits create communication breakdowns.

You have seen these bad habits at work all too often. For instance, think about the conversations you have had when other people tried to immediately change your mind or negate your point of view. They probably used words such as "You're wrong....That's not important....Yes, BUT..." Every one of these phrases automatically creates a barrier and stops an interaction between two people.

Attempting to invalidate another person's point of view or immediately change that person's mind is a common mistake many people make during conversations. Instinctively, if someone tries to change your mind before rapport is established, you resist. In effect, your resistance is your attempt to change the other person's mind about trying to change your mind. You try to sell him or her on *not* selling you.

Saying a person is wrong or challenging his thoughts creates a win-lose scenario of aggressive competitiveness. A few people actually respond to this type of aggressive response, but, in most cases, people are unable to handle having their ideas or conversations negated. Using this aggressive competitiveness type of response sets you up to lose more often than you should.

Another bad habit that causes a conversation breakdown is **analyzing the other person**, telling that individual what he or she *really* means or feels. Statements such as "What you're trying to say is...What you really mean is..." or "So, you feel worried or sad or mad or afraid..." generally cause resentment. Unless someone is paying for counseling, that person generally does not like being told how to feel or how to think. Even though some listening skill courses actually teach this technique as a way of showing understanding, the average person does not appreciate or want his or her comments analyzed.

Trying to cheer people up, or **emotionally overwhelm** them when they are at a low point, is one more way to create communication failure.

Remember the times when you were at a low point? How did you react to the enthusiastic cheerleader who said, "Oh come on...It won't be any problem at all...Don't worry about it...Cheer up. It's not so bad...." Statements such as these generally prove that the enthusiastic person has little or no understanding of the other person's situation or feelings.

Just as irritating as emotionally overwhelming a person is the conversation breaker we call **task or information overload**. This often creates analysis paralysis. Unfortunately, overpowering a person with information and tasks is all too common in today's work environment where information is easily accessible and abundant. Because most everyone has more on his to-do list than he can possibly accomplish, the natural reaction to information overload is to respond negatively or to attempt to multitask, which only increases a person's frustration and anxiety.

Other sure-fire methods of breaking rapport or stopping a conversation are **to lie, cheat, or deceive.** People respect honesty. Telling a lie or creating a deception is the fastest step toward destroying trust between two people and stopping any conversation or rapport.

Bad habits, like the five we point out here, can cause immediate communication failures. Now you know what causes conversations to stop, and you know from Chapter 3 how to use Decision Goals to initiate a conversation. The next step is the secret to keeping conversations going, and the secret to building rapport and avoiding someone saying to you, "You're not listening!"

To begin with, when people say to you, "You're not listening!" they usually mean they are not getting any acknowledgement from you. In other words, they are not getting the response that they need to show you are paying attention. When people feel that they are not being acknowledged, they usually react in one of two ways: 1) They try again, even louder, to make their points, or 2) they check out, ending the discussion. Undoubtedly, you have seen this happen many times and probably have been on both sides of these *"You're not listening"* conversations.

This chapter is designed to help you become a much more effective listener and, more importantly, give you the ability to prove to others that you indeed are listening to what is being said. We will show you how to do this and how to build and maintain rapport and to show respect for other points of view throughout your conversations.

The first step to accomplishing this is to understand the Four Rapport Acknowledgements:

100% Attention

Response

Understanding

Respect

Let us explain how building and maintaining rapport works and how to make this skill your own. Then you can decide if mastering this skill will lead you to an increase in genuine personal power with other people.

100% Attention

Giving someone your 100% attention means you listen carefully enough to determine the other person's point of view. You both listen to what the person says and watch how he says it. You also suspend all other activity – no phone calls, no emailing, no Blackberry. You literally pay attention to every word the other person says.

The paradox of doing this is that when you listen for the other person's point of view, you automatically give him your 100% attention. Being able to maintain this high level of attention with anyone, in any mood, is the crucial skill of effective listening.

As you listen, with 100% attention, remember to:

Be interested, not interesting.

Suspend all activities, including your own point of view for the moment.

Stop multitasking. (Computers are truly effective at multitasking. People are not.)

Wait until the other person is completely finished before thinking about your response.

Response

The purpose of a response acknowledgement is to prove that you are listening, that you received the message, and that the message has an impact on you. Done correctly, a response acknowledgement shows a person much more than polite words ever could convey.

By your responding to the other person, you are telling him that he has some power in the conversation. The paradox here is that the more power you give away, the more you get back because the other person knows you are the source of that power.

Here is another pointer. As you respond, do not try to be impressive. Instead, demonstrate that you are impressed. Again, the more impressed you are, the more others are impressed by you.

Basically, you have two kinds of response acknowledgements: nonverbal and verbal. Nonverbal responses include nods, facial expression of interest or concern, steady eye contact, and hand gestures. You can use these alone or combine them with verbal acknowledgements and tone of voice to reveal your sincerity.

With verbal acknowledgements, the inflection in your voice can go up or down, depending upon your response. Down acknowledgements signal that you received the message and the speaker can now change the subject or move on to another point. Sample down inflections include: *"Got it." "Thank you." "Fine." "OK."*

Up inflections signal you want the speaker to continue talking or expand on a particular point and that you are following the speaker's logic path. Up inflections include: *"Oh?" "Really?" "And..." "Then?"*

When you use response acknowledgement appropriately, you demonstrate to the speaker that he got through to you, and you eliminate any need for repetition. People appreciate having their communications acknowledged. This is true even with email and voicemail.

Not receiving a response to a message is both frustrating and annoying. Be a good communicator and acknowledge the other person by responding to his message as soon as possible, even if only to acknowledge that you received his email or voice message.

Understanding

All too often, people attempt to acknowledge others during a conversation by saying, "I understand." Unfortunately, this understanding statement is usually followed by another statement that proves the person really does not understand and has no idea what the other person meant or said. Rather than tell the other person you understand, we urge you to **prove** you understand.

You do this simply by summarizing or "netting out" what you just heard. A few words are usually sufficient. You can also ask related questions. You only need to let the other person know that you are there and, more importantly, that you got the point.

Here is a key point to remember: *Do not provide feedback to show you are listening. Do it to prove you understand.* The difference in these two intentions transmits remarkably different messages when you communicate.

Once you start proving you understand, you will soon discover that you are getting to the heart of matters faster and making quick analogies or parallels instead of delivering rote repetitions, which are common feedback techniques.

Being able to quickly and accurately net out complex messages and ideas is an executive caliber skill. When you cultivate that skill as your own, communicating and problem solving become so much easier.

Respect

To build rapport, you must prove and demonstrate respect for other people's points of view, not just proclaim respect. Just telling someone, *"I appreciate your position"* or *"I know how you feel,"* is not enough. You have to prove it. How many times has someone politely told you, "I know how you feel," and you were immediately turned off by the insincerity of the remark?

So, how does acknowledging respect work? You initiate respect by being willing to communicate with another person at his level of understanding and attitude at any moment in time. You are not being condescending. In fact, showing respect for another person is an absolute must if you are to build rapport and stay in a conversation.

There is no technique or gimmick to showing respect. You already do this with people you care about. You naturally adjust your tone of voice, rate of speech, and choice of words to show you are trying to imagine being where other people are at that moment. You do not have to be perfect at acknowledging respect, but you do have to show the other person that you are trying.

A note of caution: Respecting another person's point of view does not mean you agree with that viewpoint. Agreement and respect are not synonymous.

By acknowledging another's viewpoint, you are simply respecting the other person's right to a different point of view at this moment in time. You are not throwing your point of view away; you are just putting yours on hold while you try to understand the other person's view.

Now the good news...if your words, tone of voice, and body language communicate respect for the other person's point of view, the other three acknowledgements naturally happen. Processing the four acknowledgements while you are in conversation and trying to reach a decision can be difficult. That is why we want you to remember just one point – **Respect.** Do this and the other acknowledgements automatically occur.

Some programs on listening teach mirroring as a way for you to show respect, but mirroring is a technique and not a sign of respect. Acknowledging is more than mirroring or saying, *"I understand;"* acknowledging is a demonstration that you understand and **respect** what they say. Respect is about caring and that comes only from the heart.

Building rapport with the four acknowledgements – **100% attention, response, understanding,** and **respect** – is easy to do when you focus on what the other person is saying and not what you are going to say.

Acknowledge
Respect

- Suspend your own point of view.
- Where are they on the Ladder?
- Imagine being there yourself.
- Respond with equal energy.
- Start out with "It" or "That."
- Follow up with a question at same energy level.

COMMIT	Confident
PLAY	Enthused
CONTINUE	Interested
STUDY	Reserved
LOOK/LISTEN	Neutral
CHALLENGE	Competitive
STOP	Hostile/Opposed
AVOID	Fearful/Risk
COMPLAIN	Troubled/Sad
NEGLECT	Indifferent

Here are six pointers to help you acknowledge respect.

1. Suspend your own point of view, so you can understand the other person's position.

When you are confident about your own view, your determination to reach your goal is not going to change simply because someone else has a different viewpoint. Remember, you are not giving in or giving up when you suspend your point of view. You remain confident yet show respect for the other person.

2. Determine where the other person is on the Decision Ladder.

Being able to identify a person's emotions and attitude – at that moment in time – makes acknowledging and demonstrating respect so much easier.

You know from the clues we gave you in Chapter 2 that a person at **NEGLECT** on the Decision Ladder is going to be indifferent, not interested, or uncaring. Knowing this, you would acknowledge that indifference, and perhaps even change the subject.

What about people at **COMPLAIN**? In this case, acknowledge their frustrations, their difficulties, or their feelings of being overwhelmed.

If you realize someone is at **AVOID**, then you know that person is probably cautious, anxious, or tentative, so acknowledge the risks he or she perceives as well as any uncomfortable feelings.

Individuals at **STOP** want to block, defeat, or correct you because they feel frustrated or irritated, so acknowledge them by discontinuing your presentation and determining the reason for the **STOP**.

Someone at **CHALLENGE** will express doubts, be skeptical, or show a competitive point of view, so acknowledge that need for additional proof.

At **LOOK/LISTEN,** individuals are open to discussion, to options, and to alternatives, and are generally unbiased. Acknowledge them by presenting options or other possibilities.

When you see a person at **STUDY,** he or she will be reasonable, thorough, and cautious, so acknowledge that need to analyze, study, reason, or reflect on an idea.

The person at **CONTINUE** will be curious and ask questions, so the best way to acknowledge is simply to answer those questions.

When a person shows enthusiasm and excitement or begins to imagine possibilities or options regarding an idea, you know that he or she is obviously at **PLAY,** so acknowledge that enthusiasm and excitement.

And finally, when a person accepts your idea, or says, "Okay, let's do it," then you definitely know you are dealing with someone at the top of the Decision Ladder at **COMMIT**. The way to acknowledge is just to thank that person *for his or her commitment.*

3. Imagine being there yourself.

In other words, imagine how the other person feels at that moment in time when you interact with him or her.

Demonstrate you care, that you feel the need for more information, or feel the confusion, excitement, confidence, frustrations, or negativity.

4. Respectfully acknowledge the other person by responding to him or her with equal energy, but not always with equal volume.

Energy is the way you say your words, or the emphasis you put into your words, to let other people know that their points of view have an impact on you.

For example, if your co-worker quietly, dejectedly says to you, "I am having the worst day of my life," you would not yell back at him or her. Instead, you respond quietly but with energy.

But what about the hostile person who yells at you? Do you yell back? No, definitely not. Yelling would cause an argument, and responding meekly or mildly might even trigger the hostile person to yell more or yell louder.

Have you ever raised your voice in a customer no-service situation? A lot of people do because they think by speaking louder and stronger that the customer service representatives would hear them and pay proper attention to what they were saying.

The situation is the same when a hostile person yells at you. Instead of yelling back, let the "yeller" know that you hear him or her. Respond, with emphasis, to show that what he or she says does matter.

5. Start your sentences with *It* or *That*.

Using **It** or **That** instead of **You** both depersonalizes a conversation and shows the other person that nothing is wrong with him or her.

As a result, you have a better chance at building and maintaining rapport. Later in Chapter 6, when we discuss aligning, we will explain this depersonalization skill in greater detail.

6. Show understanding and respect for the other person by merely asking a relevant question.

Responding with a related question shows you are not only listening, but that you also are interested in what is being said.

Acknowledging is the key for open communication. After all, if you do not show respect or acknowledge the other person, how eager will that person be to talk to you about his or her own situation or issue?

As part of our PAR training, we often use a graphic to illustrate the importance of acknowledging. Our illustration consists of a circle that represents the Earth and two stick figures, one at the North Pole and one at the South Pole.

Using the graphic, we demonstrate how both stick figures yell at each other that they are UP, yet when they look around, they cannot see each other and have difficulty communicating where they are. Communication between the two can *only* happen when one of the stick figures suspends his/her perception of UP and goes to or acknowledges the other stick figure's perception of UP.

Our little stickmen could just as easily represent Democrats and Republicans and the contentious state of U.S. politics today. The two political parties have descended into yelling at each other, and they will continue doing so until someone in one of the two parties has enough confidence in his/her own position to momentarily suspend his/her view and see things from the other party's point of view. Although that rarely happens in today's political arena, when a political leader does suspend his/her own views and acknowledges the opposition, the result usually turns out to be great for the American people.

As we have pointed out, seeing a situation from another point of view is critical. A business simulation activity often used to teach the art of negotiating is another great example on the impact that acknowledging other people's viewpoints can have. In this exercise, two major companies depend on one specific type of orange to produce their products.

This rare orange only grows on one small South Pacific island. Year after year, the tiny island produces enough oranges to satisfy the demands for both companies, harvesting about 20,000 tons of oranges, with each company using 10,000 tons or half of the total production. Unfortunately, one year the island is hit by a frost that destroys fifty percent of the orange crop. The island harvests only 10,000 tons of oranges in total, which means that both companies need the entire harvest to produce their products.

In the negotiation simulation, two teams of negotiators are given the task of deciding the fate of the orange crop. Each team is told how its company uses its oranges and how many oranges are needed. The two teams negotiate to find a solution. Unfortunately, most of the simulation exercises either end in stalemates or with each company allocated 5,000 tons, which does neither company any good.

The ultimate solution only occurs when one of the negotiators asks the other company how they use their oranges. When that question is asked, the teams discover that one company uses the meat of the oranges while the other uses the rinds. Instead of each getting only half of what they need, both companies can get the part of the oranges that they need. But this win-win situation only happens if someone is confident enough to suspend his own view of reality and see the situation from another's perspective.

As this simulation exercise points out, being able to acknowledge others and respect their points of view are often critical to business success. This ability also transfers over to a person's private life as well.

A participant in one of our PAR training programs recounted how she used the acknowledgement skills learned in our classes to establish better rapport with her children. She said:

> *"Acknowledging my kids' points of view is especially difficult when I don't agree with them. However, it (PAR Rapport Acknowledgements) has done wonders for opening up the lines of communications with my sixteen-year-old."*

Another PAR participant used the four acknowledgements skills with his teenager daughter, a straight 'A' student, who was afraid that she was not Ivy League material:

> *"My first impulse was to tell her how smart she was. Then I remembered I needed to acknowledge her first, so I said, 'Ivy League schools are demanding. Why do you think you're going to have a problem?' She opened up, and we had a long conversation that ended very positively."*

Acknowledging, as these PAR participants did, creates an atmosphere of trust where others feel comfortable about revealing how they really think and feel. Only when potential followers show you their true position on the Decision Leader, can you lead. The secret to building trust is the PAR Rapport Acknowledgements.

Also, with Rapport Acknowledgements, practice does make perfect. Use the acknowledgements over and over again until they become part of your conversational style.

To help guide you with appropriate responses for each level, we have put together a list of starting points. However, we urge you not to limit yourself just to these examples. Expand your range of acknowledgements so that each one is tailored and customized to the particular point in a conversation.

Remember, however, that these sample phrases are just examples, and not scripts to be followed verbatim. More importantly, these examples will not work if you just say the words and fail to demonstrate that you care.

Examples for ACKNOWLEDGING - Part One

NEGLECT	"Sounds like it isn't a priority." "Appears that is not important." "Looks as if there are more important issues."
COMPLAIN	"That appears to be a real problem." "It must be difficult." "That sounds frustrating."
AVOID	"That looks like a real uncomfortable situation." "It appears to be risky." "Sounds like there are some things to be avoided."
STOP	"Got it. What's wrong?" "Let's stop here. What's the problem?" "Let's not go any further until we fix that."
CHALLENGE	"That's a reasonable concern." "Sounds like some proof is needed." "Skepticism is understandable."

Examples for ACKNOWLEDGING - Part Two

LOOK/LISTEN	"Glad you are open to the idea."
	"Thanks."
	"I welcome the chance to share the information with you."
STUDY	"There is a lot of information."
	"Some analysis is appropriate before proceeding."
	"Never hurts to check all the data."
CONTINUE	Just answer whatever questions are asked.
PLAY	"That does have numerous possibilities."
	"Yeah, just imagine the options."
	"I loved that also."
COMMIT	"Then let's do it."
	"Thank you for your confidence in us."
	"Based on that, I suggest we move forward with the plan."

In addition to these sample responses, occasionally it may be appropriate to add a clarifying question such as:

What are the priorities?

What's the biggest problem?

How can we avoid that risk?

What proof would be appropriate?

Where should we study first?

Well-respected business people around the globe understand the need and value of sincere rapport acknowledgements. In fact, Dr. Stephen Covey devoted a whole section of his book, *The Seven Habits of Highly Effective People*, to acknowledgements with his chapter entitled "Seek first to understand, then you will be understood."

Often, when we arrive at this point in our training sessions, many people express a serious level of discomfort, feeling that acknowledging other points of view, especially negative attitudes, puts them in a place where they do not want to be.

Those feelings would be well justified if we simply stopped with the skill of acknowledging. People who know how to acknowledge would be wonderful human beings and great to be around, but they would never be able to accomplish anything. The simple business reality is that results and accomplishments are the scorecards of success.

Rapport acknowledgement is a key component of positioning your ideas for maximum receptivity, which we will cover later in Chapter 6. So, for now, work on your ability to acknowledge all ten ACTIONS/attitudes on the Decision Ladder. We promise that being great at acknowledging will yield even bigger business results down the road to *cracking* the code.

Chapter 5

Digging Deeper

Leaders come in all sizes, ages, and walks of life. A perfect example is Steve Cauthen, a teenage jockey who made sports history when, at 17 years old, he won 447 races and then took the prestigious Triple Crown a year later. The youngest person ever admitted to horse racing's Hall of Fame, he is also the only jockey ever named *Sports Illustrated* "Sportsman of the Year."

In the magazine's "Sportsman of the Year" article featuring the teenager from Kentucky, a reporter asked Steve what his secret was to leading so many horses to first place. The young jockey explained that the first thing he did each morning was weigh himself. Every day, his weight stayed between 100 to 105 pounds. Yet, each horse he rode weighed over 1,000 pounds or more than ten times what Steve weighed.

What he realized early on as a jockey was that he could not make those horses go anyplace they do not already want to go. His job was to help them do it faster than all the other horses.

Steve Cauthen, even as a teenager, knew what successful leaders know. You cannot lead people to places they do not want to go. The real mission for leaders is to help people discover where they want to go and help them get there faster and more efficiently than they could alone.

If you are going to help people get where they want to go, then you must first understand how they see a situation, problem, or opportunity. To do this, you must ask questions, probe in depth, or literally dig deeper.

To direct people through this probing process, The PAR Group has developed a detailed question-asking procedure we call **NIQCL**. Pronounced like the word *nickel* (nĭk'əl), NIQCL guides you through the process of uncovering how others perceive or feel about a given situation.

N = NEED

I = IMPORTANCE

Q = QUANTIFY

C = CONSEQUENCES

L = LOOK/LISTEN

The first letter **N** in NIQCL stands for **N**eed, and a need is defined as either a problem or opportunity. The first step in your questioning process is to identify the problem that needs solving or opportunity that needs capturing.

The next letter **I** represents **I**mportance. With **I**mportance, you dig deeper to learn how serious, critical, or sensitive a need is and you establish the priority of the need.

Q, which stands for **Q**uantify, is used to determine the size or scope of the opportunity or problem and to identify how much and/or how often.

C represents **C**onsequences. As you probe, you ask questions to discover the effect or the consequences of what might happen if you do or do not take action. Keep in mind that consequences can be negative or positive, but when they exist, consequences stimulate change.

L is for **L**ook/**L**isten, the transition which enables you to look at all possible solutions and/or options.

NIQCL is a natural, logical discovery process used every day. In fact, you probably used NIQCL several times today, without even knowing it, as you made ordinary business and personal decisions.

Here is how NIQCL works in a real-life situation:

> *You hear an awful noise coming from the engine of your car. The loud, continuous noise sounds like a problem. (**N**eed)*

> *Your car noise sounds serious. (**I**mportance)*

> *If so, is it a $100 problem or a $900 one? (**Q**uantify)*

> *What happens if you ignore the noise? Will it go away? Get worse? Cause an accident? (**C**onsequences) Could you live with that? No! (Worse **C**onsequences)*

> *After your quick evaluation, you decide a mechanic needs to examine your car (**L**ook) and tell you what your options are. (**L**isten)*

NIQCL, as you see, is an instinctive, information-seeking process. Here's another example of NIQCL at work, but this time in a business situation. A co-worker at **COMPLAIN** comes to you and says, "We have a problem." Wanting to learn more, you undoubtedly would question him further, asking, "What's wrong?" (**N**eed); "Is it serious?" (**I**mportance); "How much?" "How often?" (**Q**uantify); "What happens if it isn't fixed?" (**C**onsequences); and then finally transition to "Got any ideas on how we can fix it?" (**L**ook/**L**isten)

Obviously you can think of dozens of instances like this when you instinctively used NIQCL to review a situation, opportunity, or problem. Now that you realize how intuitive NIQCL is, consciously using our sequence should be easy. After all, NIQCL is just a respectful way of helping others think through a situation, and a methodical way of helping you see the situation from their perspectives.

Of the five NIQCL questions, the one most overlooked or, in many cases, the one question most often not asked is **C**onsequences. Yet, knowing the consequences of an action is what usually determines the value or the willingness of a person to act or not to act.

Take dieting for example. Most everyone knows how important counting calories and carbs, limiting sugar intake, and eating right are toward healthy living. Yet, rarely does someone start living healthy or go on a diet because of long-term health reasons. The consequences of not eating healthy – i.e. a heart attack, an upcoming class reunion, a vacation to the beach, or a new bathing suit – are what usually drive someone to counting calories or adopting a healthier lifestyle.

Consequences motivate people in business, too. The Y2K computer bug is a classic business example of motivation by consequence. For three decades, information technology specialists knew that the software used by most mainframe systems had been programmed with a potential glitch that could stop those systems from working when the computers' date changed from December 31, 1999 to January 1, 2000.

Most CIOs and technology directors in the 1970s, 1980s, and a great deal of the 1990s did nothing about Y2K because the consequences and the impact of the Y2K bug were far into the future. But as the year 2000 neared, businesses realized that the consequences of not repairing the Y2K glitch could result in all computers shutting down when the date turned to January 1, 2000.

The possibility of dire Y2K consequences motivated companies, CIOs, governments, and everyday people into action. Businesses spent billions on computer software updates and upgrades to correct the Y2K bug. Worldwide, people stocked extra water and food supplies, bought generators, and kept additional cash on hand. The United States government even grounded 75% of all air traffic on January 1, 2000. People took action, but only after they understood what the consequences were and those consequences were imminent.

NIQCL helps you determine consequences. By using **N**eed, **I**mportance, and **Q**uantify, you can uncover the information you need to identify the **C**onsequences and size up a situation so that you can formulate solutions, ideas, or suggestions that will help you achieve your goal.

Here is another example of NIQCL used to probe for more information. You are assigned the job of finding out why a co-worker or employee is having a problem with a particular task. If you ask a general question such as, "How is everything?," the answer you are likely to hear is "Fine."

But what if you tried a different, more specific approach, like one of these:

> *"What are you trying to accomplish?"*
>
> *"What the biggest obstacle?" (**N**eed)*
>
> *"Is there anything else?" (**N**eed)*
>
> *"Of those two issues, which is most critical?" (**I**mportance)*
>
> *"How often does that happen? How many times a day?" (**Q**uantify)*
>
> *"How much does it cost?" (**Q**uantify)*
>
> *"What happens if that isn't fixed? Or what happens if that is fixed?" (**C**onsequences)*

Sometimes, as this conversation illustrates, you have to ask several questions to get the information you need.

Asking the NIQCL questions in order is not always necessary because the order you ask the questions is secondary to your making the interaction conversational. Remember that what you are looking for are answers to help you understand the reasons behind a person's perception or point of view.

NIQCL is the tool leaders use to learn more about their followers. For example, in almost every PAR session we conduct, a manager will ask us, "How do I motivate my people?" Each time we hear that question, we know right away that the manager who asked that does not know enough about his people, because if he did, he would KNOW what motivates his employees.

Finding out what motivates someone should only take a five- or ten-minute conversation. A What-Motivates-You conversation, one every manager should have several times a year with his team members, could go like this:

"I just wanted to take a few minutes to talk about you. What do you like about what you are currently doing?" (**N**eed)

"Have you thought about what you would like to do next?" (For new people or people just starting their new position, the goal may be to survive, but that will change as they grow accustomed to the position.) (**N**eed)

"What do you need in order to make that a reality?" (**N**eed)

"Anything else?" (**I**mportance)

"What makes sense to focus on first?" (**I**mportance)

"Have you put any numbers or scope to it yet?" (**Q**uantify)

"Once you reach that, what would that allow you to achieve?" (**C**onsequences)

"Let us look at some ways to make that happen." (**L**ook/**L**isten)

NIQCL can be especially useful for managers to gather information on motivating their associates. After all, every employee – from stockroom clerk to CEO – becomes highly motivated when he understands how a project or assignment will help him get to where he wants to go – to a higher salary, promotion, telecommuting, more responsibility, etc.

As you use NIQCL to delve deeper, remember there is a difference between scope and quantity. Also, not all information you receive from other people is easily quantifiable.

A perfect example of this occurred in one of our PAR sessions when two programmers practiced using NIQCL in a conversation.

The first programmer expressed his fear of speaking before a group at an upcoming meeting. The second programmer responded by asking, "How scared are you?" Then, he expanded hands and arms out, bit by bit, asking, "Are you this scared? Or this scared? Or this scared?"

Because fear is not easily quantifiable, a more probing conversation, one that would provide the information needed to help the soon-to-be presenter overcome his fears, might go like this:

"Have you ever presented before?" **(Q**uantify)

"How big is the group you are talking to?" **(Q**uantify)

"How long is your presentation?" **(Q**uantify)

"How well do you know the information you are presenting?" **(Q**uantify/ Scope)

"Who will be in the audience?" **(Q**uantify/ Scope)

"Do you have to demonstrate any technology?" **(Q**uantify/ Scope)

"Is your presentation being filmed?" **(Q**uantify / Scope)

As you see, these answers do more than just quantify; they allow you to ascertain the potential consequences. The consequences revealed through this interaction could help the two programmers to transition to options (**L**ook/**L**isten) that would mitigate or eliminate some of the potential speaker's fear.

When you use NIQCL for probing, your ultimate goal is to obtain the other person's point of view. Remember that you are not using your questions to influence the other person to see your viewpoint. You are probing to learn the other person's perception, and when you ask questions with this in mind, your questions have integrity.

Sometimes asking questions can sound like an interrogation, so you need to respect and acknowledge the other person's answers before asking the next question. If you fail to show respect, people will think you are trying to trap them into answers or to accept your ideas. When people sense a trap, they generally shut down and end the conversation. Respecting other people's viewpoints and acknowledging the answers they give are crucial. By doing so, you open conversations and build trust.

When used as part of conversational rapport, NIQCL helps individuals and teams solve problems productively and create teamwork with customers, associates, employees, managers, or executives. NIQCL is a proven tool that works just as well in the boardroom as it does in management meetings, on customer service calls, or on the shop floor. In fact, the more you use NIQCL in business, the more you will see that our PAR questioning process is effective in nonbusiness situations as well.

A participant in one of our training sessions recounted how the PAR probing skills had helped her at home with her eight-year-old daughter. As she was getting her daughter ready for school, her daughter suddenly said, "I don't want to go to school today because everybody always picks on me."

The mother said her first impulse was to march down to the school and find out what the problem was. Then, she remembered the discussion we had in our sessions about acknowledging and probing in some depth. Using what she had learned, the mother acknowledged and probed deeper. What she uncovered was that the day before her eight-year-old and best friend had a slight disagreement, one that probably would resolve itself at school that day. By acknowledging and probing in depth, the mother avoided a great deal of needless stress.

You can also use NIQCL as a tool for bringing people up to speed quickly on a situation. NIQCL works especially well for presenting a plan, action, or decision goal to an audience that is unfamiliar with that plan or goal.

Instead of immediately opening the presentation with a recommendation, you can utilize the NIQCL five-step process to establish a mutual perception of the needs for your solution or recommendation.

In our PAR classes, to demonstrate how NIQCL works as a guide for presentations, we use two different examples. The first illustrates how NIQCL can introduce an opportunity, and the second shows NIQCL communicating a problem.

1. OPPORTUNITY

As you know, our department has been studying opportunities for expansion into new international markets. On the basis of our research and confirmed economic projections by the U.S. State Department, we find our most interesting opportunities for the next five years to be in Canada and Brazil. (**N**eed)

Of the twenty top countries we analyzed, the most important growth markets in terms of sheer size are China, Japan, and Brazil, in that order. However, Canada and Brazil become priorities when ease of entry into the market is considered. (**I**mportance)

The numbers are impressive. Canada is approximately 10% of our domestic market, meaning $50 million in sales potential annually, based on a 12% market share. The market in Brazil is nearly the same as Canada, but Brazil has less than half the competition for our types of products and services. (**Q**uantify)

The positive consequences are more than long-term gain. Because we already have a manufacturing facility and several affiliate marketing organizations in each country, we could be operating within eighteen months.

The negative consequence of not moving now is that we risk government restrictions if our competitors move in ahead of us with manufacturing investments. That is very likely to happen in Brazil. (**C**onsequences)

So, with that in mind, what I'd like to show you today is how we could go about expanding into those markets. (**L**ook)

2. PROBLEM

Most of the potential customers coming through our call centers are booking appointments, but then they fail to show up to those appointments. These 'no-shows' are driving up costs at our locations since we are staffing our centers in expectation of the scheduled customers. (**N**eed)

Our call centers are an important aspect of new business because they represent 20% of our projected new business for this year. (**I**mportant)

If you look at the <u>numbers</u>, the booking rate is 60% of the call volume of 1,000 calls per month. Yet only 20% of the customers who book actually show up, giving us 480 no-shows. If we could double the number of customers who show up and multiply that number against the closure rate at our centers and typical sales volume – 120 customers x $4,000 x 50% closure rate x 12 months – we would experience over $2.8 million in new sales. (**Q**uantify)

However, if we do nothing, we will lose millions just on our top line. The losses are even worse when we add in the additional overhead we have in anticipation of customers that don't show up. (**C**onsequences)

I have some ideas on how we can improve call center effectiveness. Let me share them with you, and then you can decide if we should implement them. (**L**ook)

When used to present a problem, as in the above example, NIQCL brings out facts and figures that enable audiences to better analyze a situation. Without seeing the numbers multiplied and added, the audience may not see the seriousness of a problem or be open to hearing a recommendation for change.

One universal concern in business today is the inability to see situations from other points of view. However, our clients tell us that when they use NIQCL, they are better able to understand how others perceive situations or feel about an issue.

For most PAR clients, NIQCL soon becomes part of their everyday business and personal lives. They use NIQCL to analyze problems, see issues from others' points of view, and make presentations. NIQCL definitely helps them, our clients say, to evaluate options and determine how to solve problems or opportunities without creating any new problems.

To start putting NIQCL to work for you, choose an opportunity or issue currently facing you or your department. Make a NIQCL presentation using the format we have illustrated. In addition, when someone brings a problem or opportunity to you before making a judgment, use NIQCL as a tool to see the situation from that person's point of view.

Two important points to remember from this chapter are that NIQCL is a tool to use to dig deeper for facts and that the NIQCL process is an essential part of PAR's **PROBING** skills. Learning more about a person or situation, knowing a person's momentary emotion, and knowing how to establish rapport are the building blocks of the PAR skill set. Once you understand and make these **PROBING** skills your own, you are ready to move on to **ALIGNING**, which we detail in Chapter 6.

Section Three

"A" for ALIGNING

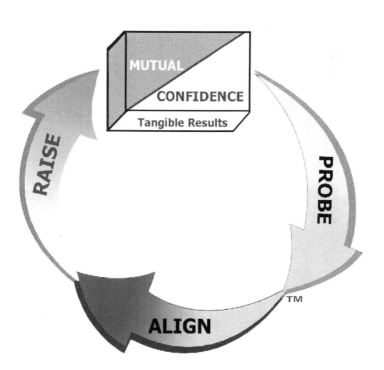

Chapter 6

Seeing from Another's Point of View

In 2001, the Xerox® Corporation faced bankruptcy. With $17 billion dollars in debt, a pending SEC scandal, and five consecutive quarters of losses, the company was in danger of imploding when Anne Mulcahy took over as CEO. The first woman ever to hold the company's coveted leadership role, Mulcahy performed what Wall Street pundits refer to as a minor miracle.

The CEO, who got her start at IBM as an entry-level field sales rep, quickly turned the company around by cutting expenses and restructuring the company's debt. In just a year, the once near-bankrupt Xerox not only reported an operating profit but was also being steered by Mulcahy into a completely new direction, from The Document Company® to consulting services and the color printer business.

"In 2002, we decided to create a global services group," explained Mulcahy in a 2006 *Fortune* magazine interview. "When I think back, those were not the most positive times at Xerox. But there is never a good time to make a strategic change. The key is to do it when the market is sending you signals, instead of waiting until your back is against the wall."

The signal for Mulcahy came from one of Xerox's customers who asked the company for help in reducing costs. Mulcahy listened to what that customer and others had to say. By probing to discover what they needed and wanted, the new CEO and Xerox were able to ALIGN their strategy and business plan with the needs of their customers.

"The skill," Mulcahy told *Fortune*, "is to stay connected to customers and to move quickly to capture the opportunity or avoid a risk."

Mulcahy and Xerox definitely captured the opportunity. By being connected and ALIGNING with their customers, Xerox became a reinvigorated, $4 billion company, and Ann Mulcahy made *Time* magazine's 2006 list of the "100 People Who Shape Our World," and recognized by *Forbes* magazine as one of the world's five most powerful women.

Effective leaders, like Anne Mulcahy, instinctively know how to connect with people and use those connections to lead others up the Decision Ladder.

Instead of pushing their points of view, leaders pay attention to how their followers view situations, and leaders offer suggestions or solutions that ALIGN with their followers' points of view.

As we pointed out in previous chapters, people listen and react based on their attitudes or feelings at a particular moment in time. People who are interested and enthused are going to see, hear, and make sense of the world quite differently from those who are hostile, troubled, or indifferent.

An important trait of successful leaders is that they realize that pushing their points of view on followers who are below neutral on the Decision Ladder is a waste of energy. People at **CHALLENGE**, **STOP**, **AVOID**, **COMPLAIN,** or **NEGLECT** filter the messages they receive with skepticism, hostility, fear, trouble, or indifference.

To be an effective leader, you must learn to respond logically to wherever a person is on the Decision Ladder, be it above or below neutral. You do this by connecting and **ALIGNING** with the other person *in the moment.*

The Decision Ladder

Degrees of In-the-Moment Motivation

ACTIONS	ATTITUDES	MEANING
COMMIT	Confident	Sure. Of Course.
PLAY	Enthused	Love it! Just imagine.
CONTINUE	Interested	What about...? (Questions)
STUDY	Reserved	Let me think about it.
LOOK/ LISTEN	Neutral	I'm open. We can discuss it.
CHALLENGE	Competitive	Yes, but... I doubt it.
STOP	Hostile/Opposed	No, you're wrong. Forget it.
AVOID	Fearful	I'm not sure. It is risky.
COMPLAIN	Troubled	Too much of a problem.
NEGLECT	Indifferent	Why bother. Not interested.

(+) Accepting

Any Idea or Information (– Neutral)

Non Accepting (–)

©1980-2007

To ALIGN with people of varying attitudes, simply apply common sense and react logically. For instance, what would you do if the person you are talking to is not interested (**NEGLECT**) at all in what you have to say? You probably would just thank him for his time and find someone else who is interested. What about that co-worker who thinks your idea is difficult or complex (**COMPLAIN**), but you want her to buy-in? Would you not make an effort to find a way to simplify your idea and see if she could buy-in to that approach?

ALIGNING can be easy and intuitive. Test yourself to see how you would respond or **ALIGN** in these other business situations. *(See our suggested responses on the bottom of this page.)*

1. *If someone thinks your idea is potentially risky (**AVOID**), you would look for ways to make it what?*

2. *If someone thinks your way is definitely wrong and not going to work (**STOP**), what would you do?*

3. *If someone is skeptical about your idea (**CHALLENGE**), how would you react?*

4. *If someone is open to considering your approach (**LOOK/LISTEN**), what would you do?*

5. *If someone wants to think about and analyze your approach (**STUDY**), what action would you take?*

6. *If someone asks questions (**CONTINUE**), what would you do?*

7. *If someone is picturing the possibilities and likes what you presented (**PLAY**), how would you respond?*

8. *If someone reaches confidence and commits to your plan (**COMMIT**), what would you do next?*

ANSWERS

1. *Make it less risky.* 2. *Find out why and prevent the potential problem.* 3. *Offer proof.* 4. *Tell them more.* 5. *Give them time and space to think it through.* 6. *Answer all their questions.* 7. *Thank them.* 8. *Get started on implementation.*

Real life, obviously, is not always as simplistic as the situations we outlined. Yet, being able to **ALIGN** with another person's emotions or attitudes is not hard to do. After all, **ALIGNING**, the logical side of empathy, is simply suggesting what makes sense in any given situation.

However, before you can **ALIGN**, you must **PROBE** to determine where someone is on the Decision Ladder. First, acknowledge respect for the person's point of view, and then ask questions, if necessary, to determine how the person sees the situation or issue. Once you know the person's attitude, you **ALIGN** with that person by looking for ways to offer a suggestion that fits the person's point of view so that you stay in the conversation and move toward your goal.

PROBING also helps you uncover information that your followers may know that you do not know. The feedback or information you receive from them becomes invaluable as you formulate your **ALIGNING** strategy and, ultimately, reach your leadership goal.

We developed a set of response guidelines to help steer you through the **ALIGNING** process and deal with each level on the Decision Ladder. Clearly, having a ready response to everything you could possibly hear when you interact with others is impossible. Undoubtedly, you will encounter situations when an **ALIGNED** solution is not immediately evident. When this happens, maintain your confidence and ask more questions which will help you better understand the other person's perspective. Eventually, a solution will become apparent.

Remember the point of **ALIGNING** is to remain in the conversation so that you engage the other person and lead him or her up the Decision Ladder to confidently commit to your point of view.

Decider's ACTION	Decider's ATTITUDE	Guidelines for ALIGNING
COMMIT	Confident	Quickly "net out" your message. Speak with decisive conviction. Get a decision. Draw a conclusion. State your beliefs.
PLAY	Enthused	Enjoy the moment. Play back. Let the Decider talk. He/She is likely to suggest the next appropriate decision.
CONTINUE	Interested	Pursue questions and answer briefly. Stay at high interest by asking for other questions. Do not go down the Decision Ladder.
STUDY	Reserved	Discuss facts – how they make sense, how the idea is reasonable or realistic. Use words like *study, conservative,* or *moderate.* Do not use superlatives.
LOOK/ LISTEN	Neutral	Explain in a relaxed manner. Explain how you or the Decider can look at relevant information – look at things now, how they used to be, how they might be. Ask if he/she would like to see or listen to the prevailing points of view; have others take a look; conduct a trial, and make observations; hear what others have said about your ideas or take one step at a time.

CHALLENGE	Competitive	The **CHALLENGE** is to find the best option for the specific situation at hand, even if it is not the usual best way for most situations. This is the time to be competitive by offering proof or testing assumptions.
STOP	Hostile	Immediately acknowledge. Use response acknowledgments, such as "Got it!" Focus attention on details through probing questions. Figure out how your ideas or solutions can be explained in terms of stopping something undesirable.
AVOID	Fearful	Explain how your idea might help avoid something. Usually, your idea can be explained in terms of helping the listener **AVOID** problems. If it cannot, ALIGN by offering to help figure out some **AVOID** strategies.
COMPLAIN	Troubled	Acknowledge the other person's attitude by saying "*It sounds like a problem.*" Then, explain how your idea might help. When people are troubled, they are asking for just one thing – HELP. They seldom can believe that instantly you are going to make their problem disappear... even if you could!
NEGLECT	Indifferent	Temporarily change the subject. Find out what the person is interested in. Come back to your subject later when there is higher rapport in the conversation.

Sailing with PAR skills

ALIGNING is sometimes easier to understand when used in nonbusiness situations. Take this example for instance. You live on Island A and have received an invitation to dinner on Island B. You plan to travel on your small sailboat, your only mode of transportation, to the other island. But, which way should you sail to Island B?

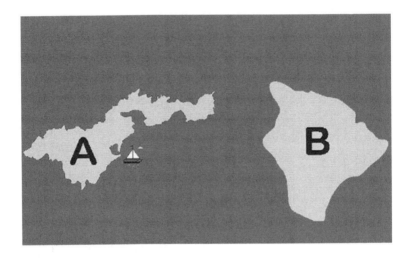

Obviously, the answer is straight 90 degrees due east. But what if strong winds are blowing from the Northeast? Sailing straight ahead would cause you to miss both the island and your dinner.

So, you change your strategy, and instead of going straight, you tack to reach the island. But, what if the strong winds are from the Southeast? You would tack differently. And if gale force winds are blowing directly in your face? Under these circumstances, sailing straight ahead may not be the wisest decision.

You could tack back and forth to reach Island B, but you would have to leave earlier than originally planned to reach the island in time for dinner. Or you could lower the sails and use the boat's motor to travel to the other island. As the situation changes, your strategy changes. The answer then to our question about which way to sail from Island A to B is "*It depends.*"

When we present this scenario to our classes, we usually get a variety of different suggestions, ranging from inviting the host on Island B to Island A for dinner to canceling dinner all together. One truly creative participant suggested a unique alternative, noting that because this is a really small planet, the person could sail around the world reaching Island B from the other side!

As that PAR participant did, you need to be creative at times when trying to **ALIGN**. Unfortunately, not many people or organizations use their creativity when they should. Too often businesses, managers, and others box themselves into a limited number of solutions. Their agendas block their creativity and hamper their abilities to reach their goals.

What about your creativity? Do you have blocks or limits on how creative you can be? Check your creativity with this connect-the-dots puzzle. First, draw nine dots, three rows of three dots, on a piece of paper (as in the illustration across). Next, starting at any dot, connect all nine dots. You may cross lines, but:

   1. *You may not use more than four straight lines.*

   2. *You may not lift your pen/pencil off the paper once you start.*

   3. *You may not retrace lines.*

●   ●   ●

●   ●   ●

●   ●   ●

Most people try to solve this puzzle by working inside the imaginary box formed by the eight dots that make up the perimeter or outside of the diagram.

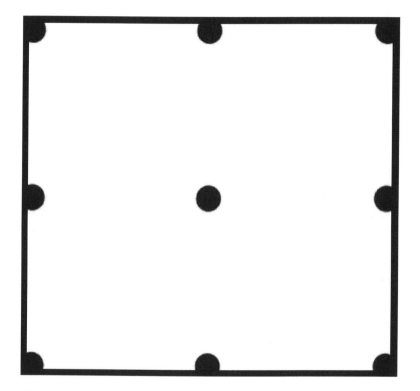

But there is no box...only three rows of dots. As long as you confine yourself to the boundaries of the imaginary box, you cannot solve the puzzle. The solution and success are found only when you creatively think outside the box. (Now you know where the phrase, *"Think outside the box,"* originated.)

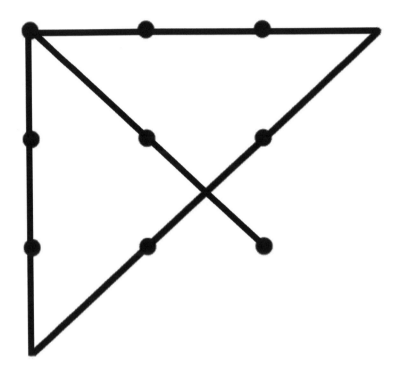

When we show people the solution, we usually hear groans which are quickly followed by, "Of course." The out-of-the-box solution is painfully obvious when revealed.

Here's another creativity exercise using the same nine-dot puzzle. This time, however, your challenge is to connect all nine dots with one straight line. Can you do it? Can you think outside the box?

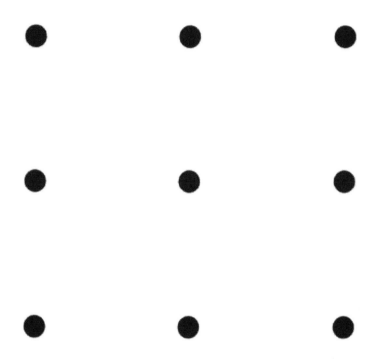

The simplicity of the solution will surprise you, but you are going to have to wait to find out how to creatively connect these dots. Look for the answer at the end of this chapter.

Being able to think outside the box is so important to being a successful leader. To **ALIGN** with another person and reach your goals, oftentimes, you have to be creative and consider alternative ideas or actions.

Back in Chapter 3, we focused on Decision Goals and the difference between goals/objectives and strategy/plans. A goal/objective is where you are going while a strategy/plan is the roadmap that guides you there. The difference between the two is key if you are a leader trying to **ALIGN** with people with Negative attitudes.

When dealing with Negative attitudes, you must stay focused on your goal and realize that people with Negative attitudes are NOT rejecting you or your goal. Their negativity is mostly directed at the plan and/or strategy for the goal. In other words, what they are resisting is the **IT** (the plan/strategy) and not **YOU**. If you look at Negative attitudes this way, you can maintain the confidence necessary to acknowledge and **ALIGN** with even the most emotional Negative attitudes.

When responding to people who are at Negative, instead of saying, "I know how you feel," "You sound frustrated," or "You seem skeptical," take the **YOU** out of your response and refer to the issue or situation as **IT**. Use phrases such as "That appears to be a problem," "It can be frustrating," or "Skepticism is perfectly understandable."

Switching pronouns from **YOU** to **IT** may seem like a small thing now, but in a leadership interaction, this simple act is extremely powerful in helping your followers separate themselves from the problem at hand. Utilizing terms such as **I** and **YOU** often creates a competitive win/lose battle, causing problems to become internalized.

Using **IT** puts the focus on issues and concerns. Instead of problems becoming people problems, you turn all issues and problems into an **IT**. By removing **YOU** from the discussion and triangulating from **YOU** and **ME** to **IT**, all issues and problems turn into an **IT** and **ALIGNING** starts.

Take a look at these examples of how a triangulated statement removes the **YOU** from the problem at each of the four Negative levels on the Decision Ladder:

ATTITUDE/ Response Level	A TRIANGULATED Statement	vs. a YOU Statement
Competitive	1. *"It appears that needs to be improved, so..."*	1. *"You doubt what I said."*
Hostile	2. *"It sounds like that's got to be stopped, so..."*	2. *"You don't like the idea."*
Fearful	3. *"It looks risky in that case, so..."*	3. *"Why are you afraid?"*
Troubled	4. *"It seems like a difficult situation, so..."*	4. *"You are upset about it."*

©1980-2007

Effective leaders are skillful at **PROBING** and **ALIGNING** to every level on the Decision Ladder from the positives to the negatives. When a follower is at Neutral or higher, most leaders find that they can easily **PROBE** and **ALIGN**. After all, doing business with people who are open to ideas is simple and simpler still when people agree with those ideas.

However, the hallmark of a strong leader is being able to influence a discussion when the conversation turns negative. In the real world of business, you will encounter the full range of negative perspectives, from **CHALLENGE** to **NEGLECT**. Your personal and professional success hinges on your ability to **ALIGN** with those perspectives as competently as you do with the higher points of view of **STUDY**, **CONTINUE**, **PLAY,** and **COMMIT**.

As you perfect your **ALIGNING** skills, use our two-part **ALIGNING** aid as a guide:

P **R** **O** **B** **E**	• Recognize where the follower is on the Decision Ladder. • Acknowledge respect. • Triangulate all issues and problems. • If needed, ask questions.(NIQCL)
A **L** **I** **G** **N**	• Offer a suggestion that fits the situation and is productive in reaching your goal. • Let's look/discuss options.

One way to better understand how **ALIGNING** fits in the overall PAR leadership process is to compare our PAR skills to sailing. Take the sailboat's flag at the top of a sailboat's mast. That flag lets sailors know which way the wind is blowing. Our Decision Ladder lets leaders know the current attitude of their potential followers.

Successful sailors respect and acknowledge the power of the wind, just as successful leaders respect and acknowledge their followers' points of view.

At times, sailors need to know more than just the direction of the wind, so they seek additional information such as barometric pressure, wind speed, dew point, and weather forecasts. Leaders often need more in-depth information to understand a problem or opportunity, so they **PROBE** and ask NIQCL questions.

Sailors position their sails to maximize the power of the wind. Leaders position their ideas to maximize the power of their followers' emotions. Sailors know that the wind can change speed and direction at a moment's notice, so they constantly monitor conditions and adjust or **ALIGN** their sails as needed. Knowing that attitudes are momentary, leaders monitor their perspective followers and realign as needed.

Here is another tip that might help if you are having difficulty **ALIGNING**. The problem, most of the time, when you see that **ALIGNING** is not working, is that you need to know more about the situation. You need to uncover more facts and feelings. The quick and easy solution is to **PROBE** deeper. If you have treated your potential followers with respect, they will give you multiple opportunities to **ALIGN** or position your idea in a way that makes sense to them.

If you ever reach a point in **ALIGNING** when you have no idea where to go with your probing question, a great plan B is simply to say, "I'm lost. Help me understand the situation better." Leaders are never too proud to ask potential followers for help in getting to where they both want to go.

In the romantic comedy, *Jerry Maguire*, the lead character, sports agent Jerry Maguire (played by Tom Cruise), is in grave danger of losing his only client, football star Rod Tidwell (Cuba Gooding). Jerry needs help **ALIGNING** with Rod. Preparing for a critical meeting with his client, Jerry frantically rehearses the one line he intends to use – "Help me, help you."

That classic movie line summarizes the importance of **PROBING** and **ALIGNING**. In other words, if you have trouble **ALIGNING**, do as Jerry Maguire did, and ask your followers to "Help me, help you."

Over time and with practice, you will develop your own responses to deal with each attitude on the Decision Ladder. To help you start, we put together sample responses and suggestions for each level.

1. "No point in covering that. I don't use it, and I don't think anybody else actually needs it either." (NEGLECT/Indifferent)

ALIGNED Response: *"It seems like this application may not be a good fit right now. What are your other priorities?"* (As we previously indicated, **ALIGNING** with neglect is often difficult or impossible.)

2. "Gee, I'd like to help, but I need help myself right now. I can't even look at another problem. I've got all this work to finish by Friday, and I just don't think that is enough time. I don't know what I'm going to do. It's a mess." (COMPLAIN/Troubled)

ALIGNED Response: *"It sounds like there's a lot to do in a short time and adding to that might cause more of a problem. So, what probably makes sense is to find a way to lighten that load or perhaps get some assistance for you on those other projects. Would that help?"*

3. "I'm not sure. Why don't you ask Pete? Maybe he'd like to work on this. Maybe he would prefer to work with someone else. You know." (AVOID/Fearful)

ALIGNED Response: *"I gather that this is an uncomfortable situation. So, to avoid that, it might make sense to handle this carefully with everyone up front, including Pete. Why don't you and I talk to him first just to check and be on the safe side?"*

4. "Wrong. You might as well take me off this job right now, because if that production line speeds up, it will cause all kinds of problems, and I refuse to be responsible. And don't say I didn't warn you about the problems it's going to cause." (STOP/Hostile)

ALIGNED Response: *"It sounds like this is a mistake, a bad mistake. So, if we are going to do it right, let's stop right now and fix the flaws before launching the increased production schedule. Fill me in on the most critical issues."*

5. "Are you serious? You want me to accept it sight unseen? I don't know if I can even use it." (CHALLENGE/Competitive)

ALIGNED Response: *"Apparently more proof is needed before we can seriously consider this suggestion. So, the initial challenge is to prove it has merit and can be applied in our environment. I'm ready to put it to the test right now."*

6. "Well, it might be an opportunity to take what's available now, who knows. So, I'm open to it. It would help if we could discuss it more." (LOOK, LISTEN/Neutral)

ALIGNED Response: *"Thanks for your openness. Let's get together this afternoon to talk over the details and review all the data."*

7. "Well, it seems to me that there is a lot of information and data to consider. I need some more time to get my head around all this information for each of the proposals before going any further." (STUDY/Reserved)

ALIGNED Response: *"There are a lot of details to consider before reaching a conclusion. So, what might make sense is to take the time now to review each proposal to make certain they are complete. It might cut down on our study time if we did the review together."*

8. "That sounds good. How did you get a budget for that? When do you start and how quickly will it be up to full production?" (CONTINUE/Interested)

ALIGNED Response: *"Initially I prepared a well-justified budget request and presented it to the CFO. Then we got the approval of the executive committee. Initial test runs will start within the next 60 days, and full production is scheduled for the beginning of the new fiscal year. What else would you like to know?"*

9. "This is a great idea, and it has numerous applications beyond the initial training phase. I can envision long-term contracts with multi-phase reinforcement opportunities." (PLAY/Enthused)

ALIGNED Response: *"It is certainly an exciting concept and not only does it open up long-term engagements, but it could also cause the referral business to double over the next 18 months."*

10. "Fine. That's easy enough. I'll take care of it. Send me a summary of the key points, and I'll handle it." (COMMIT/Confidence)

ALIGNED Response: *"Thanks. I appreciate the support. I'll have the summary on your desk by the close of business today."*

Keep in mind these are only sample responses designed to give you the feel for the two parts of an **ALIGNED** response: 1) Acknowledge, and then 2) Use the appropriate action strategy to **ALIGN**. More than personally relating to people, **ALIGNING** is relating information to people so that the decision-making process moves forward.

Another key point to remember is that when you work with people at NEGLECT, you can either accept their indifference for that moment or change the subject, hoping to find out what is important to that person and discovering other ways to present your idea. Occasionally, you may find yourself in a situation where you need a decision and cannot accept the person's indifference. In those rare cases, do not even attempt to **ALIGN** – go straight to **COMMIT** and stay there. Eventually something higher than **NEGLECT** will come back from the decider, and when that happens, you **PROBE** and **ALIGN** using that new attitude.

Being perfectly **ALIGNED** to each attitude is not always necessary. All you need to do is get close. This is especially true when a person displays mixed emotions.

For example, if you sense a person is between **COMPLAIN** and **AVOID**, adopt an empathetic position which closely relates to either attitude. If the person responds to that, you know you are close enough to still be in communication. If not, you missed, so simply try again.

ALIGNING requires creativity and acceptance. If you stereotype character or personality types or start judging attitudes as good/bad, right/wrong, you will miss countless opportunities to **ALIGN** with momentary changes. After all, momentary change is what leadership is all about. And, a person's point of view changing from subject-to-subject is what makes leadership possible and teamwork desirable.

Now that you know how to **ALIGN**, we recommend you practice so that **ALIGNING** becomes a natural part of your leadership skill set. To get started, try these four exercises:

Watch two people who respect each other work together. Then watch two people who don't respect each other work together. Which situation do you see evidence of **ALIGNMENT**?

Observe a group presentation. What is the **ALIGNING** strategy? Does the speaker **ALIGN** to the audience, or try to make the audience **ALIGN** to him/her?

The next time you are in a situation where a proposed change does not really suit you, do this:

Carefully identify the modification you want.

Find out the ideas and feelings of the people who created the proposed change.

Develop an **ALIGNED** strategy to position your suggestion.

Present your suggestion to those who proposed the change in an **ALIGNED** manner.

Think of a person with whom you have the most difficulty *"getting through"* to or communicating. How much time or effort do you spend **ALIGNING** with that person? How much effort would that person say you spend? No rule dictates that you have to **ALIGN** with or even communicate with everybody. You can fix the situation if you wish or leave it alone. Choosing to **ALIGN** or not depends on what kind of result you want.

ALIGNING is the transition from following to leading. As you perfect your **ALIGNING** skills, you can build that bridge from where your followers are, to where you and they would like to be. Effective **ALIGNING** is an absolute requirement prior to learning how to take the lead, which we explain in Chapter 7.

Before we move on to the next chapter, as we promised, here is the solution for the nine-dot puzzle. Take the paper with the nine dots, fold it so that all nine dots are on top of each other, and then stick your pen/pencil through the paper. Now you have one straight line. How is that for *thinking outside the box!*

Section Four

"R" for RAISING

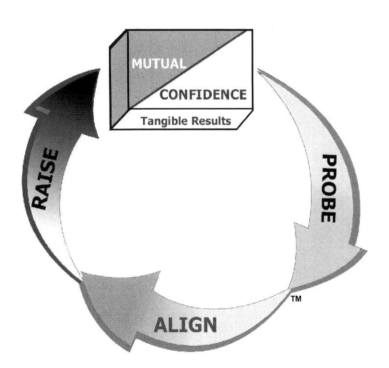

Chapter 7

Sailing the Course

Martin Luther King, Jr., Mother Teresa, Winston Churchill, John F. Kennedy, Gandhi, and Nelson Mandela. All of these people have one thing in common. They were leaders, and the world knew they were leaders for one simple reason: They had followers.

For decades, pundits have said that leadership is intangible and not measurable. But all one has to do is look at MLK, Jr., Mother Teresa, Churchill, or any other leader to see that leadership is clearly measurable. Leaders are determined by their followers. No followers, no leader. Simply put: A leader is someone who has a follower.

Leadership, in fact, is merely getting wholehearted followers for a given course of action. Leadership does not have to be a world-changing event and whether you realize it or not, you have demonstrated leadership skills countless times throughout your life.

If you are married, you have demonstrated leadership. If you have convinced others to join you in a civic project, you demonstrated leadership. If you presented an idea, no matter how large or small, that others implemented at your workplace, you demonstrated leadership. Coincidently, the skill you used in these instances is the same skill that recognized leaders in business, government, and public and private sectors use to obtain followers.

Leadership power is generally derived from three sources:

The Power of Position

The Power of Economics

The Power of Influence

When people talk about leaders, inevitably someone mentions infamous dictators such as Hitler and Saddam Hussein. After all, they had followers, so they were leaders.

Hitler and Saddam used fear and the power of their positions to gain followers. Similarly, some business leaders today lead their organizations using their power of position or power of economics.

Unfortunately, that kind of leadership seldom lasts because positional and economic powers are limited and often result in surrender or compliance. Those limitations were apparent in the rise of worker unions in the United States during the 1800s.

Back then, workers organized to counteract the abuses of positional and economic power by many business leaders. This adversarial relationship, which continued through the 20th century, only receded in recent years when business and union leaders realized that the skill of influencing each other is much more effective than a strike or a lockout.

The only true, unlimited source of a leader's power is the ability to influence potential followers. As an ancient Chinese philosopher once said, "The true measure of leadership is when followers get to their goal and believe they did it themselves."

What is important to know about the power of influence is that this power is available to all of us and its potential is unlimited. One does not have to be a CEO, a president, or a general to influence others and be recognized as a leader. Leadership occurs at all levels of an organization – from the executive suite down to the shop floor – and at every level in between. Influential leaders, no matter what title they have or role they play, are those with *willing* followers.

By now, you are probably thinking, *"Okay, I understand what leadership is, but how do I lead?"* That is the purpose of this chapter. As we pointed out earlier, you have already demonstrated the ability to influence others and, therefore, lead. Now, we are going to show you how to enhance that skill so that it becomes a conscious competence that you can use at will.

But first, we need to dispel the myth that leadership is doing something to other people. In fact, effective leadership is something you do to YOURSELF. You make yourself easy to follow, and others will willingly follow.

In our previous chapters, we discussed the essential communication skills that effective leaders use. First, leaders establish a common goal for a leadership interaction. Next, they read their potential followers in the head and heart, acknowledge the others' points of view (even when they do not agree with them), and use NIQCL to clarify the facts. Then leaders position their ideas so they make sense to potential followers. Once aligned with their potential followers, effective leaders are ready to take the lead and inspire their audiences to follow them.

To better understand the process of inspiring others, let us look at a time when you reached a confident commitment to an idea. You probably started with openness to the idea (**LOOK/LISTEN**). Then you gathered data and facts and determined how the idea would work and what it would do (**STUDY**).

At some point, the idea became truly interesting, so you delved deeper for more specific information. You considered the advantages and why your approach was functionally better (**CONTINUE**). Next, you actually imagined how your idea would work if implemented and pictured the outcome or results (**PLAY**). Then, finally, you decided to go for it and take your idea public (**COMMIT**).

Now, apply this same decision process to an actual situation. In this case, assume you need a new car. Your initial reaction to a new car purchase could place you anywhere on the Decision Ladder, but for this example, assume that you *need* to buy a car.

Knowing you need a car, you look at what vehicles are available, and because you have not purchased a car in a while, you consider several different makes and models (**LOOK/LISTEN**).

After daydreaming of owning a sports car, you get down to reality, determining how you will use your new car. How much car can you afford? Does the car need to be roomy enough for your family? How important is fuel economy? Will you take the car on long trips or use it just in town?

These and other considerations form the starting point for your car purchase. Then, as you narrow your search and work towards a decision, you might research a number of different vehicles and manufacturers, consult consumer reports, or even search the Internet for car facts and comparisons (**STUDY**).

Once you determine the make and model you want, you visit a dealership, see the car, and ask the salesperson questions. You may even look at other cars on the lot or compare the financial advantages of buying a used car or last year's model (**CONTINUE**).

When all your questions are answered and you have the facts you need, your next step might be picturing yourself driving the particular car you have in mind. Or you may even take a test-drive to feel how the car handles on the road (**PLAY**).

And, in the end, feeling confident about which car best fits your needs, you make your decision and buy the car (**COMMIT**).

This step-by-step process is how important decisions are made and probably how you arrive at the important decisions in your life – from buying a house or car to joining an organization to taking the promotion or accepting a new job assignment.

Stop for a minute and think about the last big decision you made. If your friends or family were to ask you how you arrived at your conclusion, you probably would walk them through this exact decision process.

This is also what effective leaders do to influence potential followers to buy-in and co-own plans, ideas, goals, etc. Leaders simply reveal their own motivations, and by doing so, they make it easier for others to commit to a common course of action.

The key is to understand that you cannot lead anyone any higher than where you are on the Decision Ladder. Does this mean that leadership requires that you be fully committed to an idea before you can inspire others up the Decision Ladder? Not necessarily.

For instance, you are a team leader with a promising marketing proposal, but you are not fully committed to the idea. You are, however, committed to further **STUDYING** the idea and, therefore, could inspire your team to analyze and investigate further. Additional **STUDY** on the idea would help everyone, including you, reach the commitment necessary to roll out the new product or service.

Another important point to note here is a follower seldom goes beyond **STUDY** and **CONTINUE** without being presented a solid business case. Decisions are based on both facts and feelings, and facts are presented on the Decision Ladder at **STUDY** and **CONTINUE**.

Without receiving the details or the information needed, a follower will not fully understand an idea or be able to picture the results.

We see this happen with many of our clients. New ideas and strategies fail to gain traction because potential leaders are unable to present a solid business case for their ideas at **STUDY** and **CONTINUE**.

As a result, the potential followers, even though they may think an idea is good, do not have the information they need to make a decision, and nothing happens. No results take place. Ideas stagnate. New strategies go nowhere.

Sometimes an employee's enthusiasm for an idea gets in the way of the facts. Too often, when presenting an idea or plan to an executive, an employee is so enthusiastic that he or she fails to give the details the executive needs to think through the idea. Instead of presenting facts, the employee acts like the excited child who wants to take action but is too wound up to tell why or how the conclusion was reached.

Giving followers the facts they need is crucial, so they can comfortably move beyond **STUDY** and **CONTINUE** to the next levels. Trying to get followers to go to **PLAY** or **COMMIT** without facts generally leads to frustration.

A classic example of facts and feelings working together in business is the story of the birth of the legendary Ford Mustang.

The year was 1960, Lee Iacocca was the new General Manager for the Ford Division, and Ford was developing the Cardinal, a new German-built compact car. After just a few months in his new job, Iacocca realized that the Cardinal was not a good idea. The compact car probably would work in the European market, but the Cardinal, Iacocca believed, had little or no chance in the United States of reaching Ford's projected sales goal of 300,000 units.

Iacocca went to Ford's senior management with his views, and according to his autobiography, the executives "were only too pleased to have a young upstart like me take direct responsibility, if stopping the Cardinal turned out to be a gigantic mistake."[1] In this instance, Iacocca read the management team, his audience, at **AVOID**, and he minimized their risks. He led; they followed.

With the Cardinal out of the way, Iacocca and his team were free to develop ideas for their own car (**LOOK/LISTEN**). To get started, they identified and researched the demographics of their target market, the coming-of-age Baby Boomer generation. The Ford team learned that over the next decade these Boomers, between 18 to 34 years old, would be better educated than any previous generation and would account for more than 50% of the increase sales in all new cars sold.[2]

This initial research (**STUDY**) inspired Iacocca and his team to investigate deeper into the Baby Boomers and what they wanted in an automobile. Early **STUDIES** showed the Boomers wanted "great styling, strong performance and a low price,"[3] and follow-up research revealed the appropriate styling details and the wide range of options that would appeal to Ford's broadest customer base. Again, Iacocca led, and others followed.

Unfortunately, Iacocca and his team faced two major stumbling blocks. First, could the company afford the $300 to $400 million needed to develop the car from the ground up, and second, how soon could they introduce their new car? To overcome those obstacles, the Iacocca team focused on ways to save money, which they did by using components already in the system (**CONTINUE**), and cutting the time to market in half by using an existing platform[4] (**CONTINUE**).

Next, they built a prototype, so the people at Ford could imagine (**PLAY**) what the finished car would look like, and imagine they did. "Henry Ford II came by one day to have a look," writes Iacocca in his autobiography. "He climbed into the car and announced, 'It's a little tight in the back seat. Add another inch for leg room.' "[5] (**COMMIT**)

The rest of the story is history. Introduced on April 17, 1964, at the New York World's Fair, the Ford Mustang sold 418,812 cars in the first year and generated $1.1 billion dollars (1964-66 dollars) in net profits in the first two years. Four decades and nine generations of Mustangs later, the car is still a Ford best seller.

Iacocca led, and the Ford Motor Company followed him to great success. Along the journey to his goal, Iacocca reached various levels of commitment. First was his commitment that the Cardinal was wrong for the U.S. market. Then, he committed to **LOOKING** and **LISTENING** to other options, committed to **STUDYING** the car-buying market, committed to **CONTINUING** down avenues that seemed promising, committed to **PLAYING** with the best versions, and finally he **COMMITTED** to building the Mustang.

Iacocca's big decision was made easier by the small decisions he made along the way. Iacocca talked himself up the Decision Ladder, and others willingly followed. In other words, Iacocca **RAISED** himself up the Decision Ladder, and his followers followed all the way to **COMMIT**.

RAISING is a skill that you use to influence others to commit to an action. You do not have to be an Iacocca, head of a billion-dollar company, or a world leader to **RAISE**. You could be a project manager looking to bring the project in on time and under budget; a salesperson wanting to lead a qualified prospect to become a satisfied customer; a newly promoted department supervisor needing greater commitment from your associates; a branch office manager seeking a larger budget from corporate headquarters; a stressed-out small-business owner looking for a better way to balance work life and personal life; or a harried committee chairman seeking commitment and help organizing a special event for the community.

No matter what your role or situation may be, **RAISING** will work for you just as it worked for Iacocca in the 1960s and as it works today for the half a million or more people we have trained.

The primary rule to remember about **RAISING** is that you must be **COMMITTED** to an idea in order to take your audience all the way to **COMMIT**. You cannot have an idea you merely "like." You must have confidence and conviction in your idea at each of the four positive levels of the Decision Ladder: Neutral (the possibilities/options), Reserved (the facts), Interested (the advantages), and Enthused (the satisfying outcomes).

Effective leaders, whether an Iacocca, a project manager, or a salesperson, are confident and committed to their ideas at all levels. More importantly, leaders know how to talk about their ideas from every viewpoint needed to **RAISE** because they have already been there and experienced that point of view.

PAR is *invitational* leadership. You lead and invite others to follow to the biggest decision they can commit to today. In other words, the essence of your being able to lead is your capacity to **RAISE** yourself up the Decision Ladder to the highest level the Decider (your audience) is willing to go in a conversation. This is how invitational leadership works.

We are sure that no one has ever told you that to lead you had to first invite others to follow because no one has ever taught leadership this way before. Instead, most leadership books you read or the classes you attended focused on a set of tactics and steps that you practiced on others. As you probably discovered, those tactics and steps that worked so well in role playing lose their luster when applied to real business situations.

The key distinction is that with **RAISING** or invitational leadership, the other person is the one who chooses to move to a higher viewpoint on the Decision Ladder. You cannot force others up the Ladder; they move on their own will and convictions. And you already know this because this is how you were successful in your past better moments.

How do you determine if others are following and joining you at higher levels on the Decision Ladder? You **PROBE**, constantly monitoring the others' positions on the Decision

Ladder and observing *HOW* they respond, their body language, their tone of voice, and the actions they take at that moment in time.

As you **PROBE**, ask yourself, "Are they open to possibilities? Do they appear to be thinking through your idea? Are they asking questions? Are they picturing the possibilities? Have they decided to join you?" Watch for **LOOK/LISTEN**, **STUDY**, **CONTINUE**, **PLAY,** and **COMMIT**.

PAR is not a set of steps, but a single interlinked skill with **P**ROBE-**A**LIGN-**R**AISE forming a continuous ring much like a rotary engine constantly spinning in a circular motion.

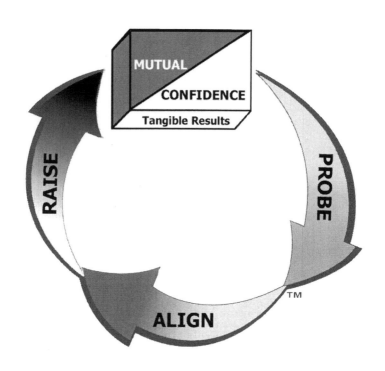

MUTUAL
CONFIDENCE
Tangible Results

RAISE

PROBE

ALIGN

™

PAR LEADERSHIP MODEL

As you **RAISE**, you constantly monitor or **PROBE** where your audience is on the Decision Ladder and **ALIGN** appropriately before continuing to **RAISE**.

What happens if you **RAISE** and people do not immediately follow? Go back and **ALIGN** again. Thorough **ALIGNING** precedes successful **RAISING**. Trying to **RAISE** without first **ALIGNING** is quite uncomfortable. A helpful way to think of **RAISING** is that when you **RAISE**, you are realigning your ideas to more positive attitude levels on the Decision Ladder. People follow because they are voluntarily **ALIGNING** to those higher points of view, and they are moving in a direction they want to go to reach well-informed decisions.

PROBE-**A**LIGN-**R**AISE is the skill set that separates leaders from people who cannot implement change. If you can **P**ROBE-**A**LIGN-**R**AISE, you will succeed in business and in your personal life because you are able to gather support from others. After all, a team is stronger than any individual, and that is why leadership is so valuable.

In Chapter 3, we referred to the story of Billy Payne and the pivotal role he played in bringing the 1996 Olympic Games to Atlanta. This is also a perfect example of being committed to an idea, gathering support from others, and influencing them to take action.

Billy Payne was a lawyer-turned-real estate salesman living in Athens, Georgia, about 45 miles from Atlanta, when his Olympic quest began in 1987. On a winter Sunday in a special service at his church, Payne watched the congregation joyously celebrate paying off a $2.5 million building loan. Energized by the enthusiasm and commitment he just witnessed, he began thinking of ways to expand that enthusiasm beyond his church to the people of Georgia. For the next few days, he tossed around several different plans, until the idea of bringing the Olympic Games to Atlanta hit him.

Atlanta's hosting the Games definitely intrigued him, not just because of the endless possibilities of the idea, but also because of the excitement and energy that the Games would offer the city and Georgia. At this point, Payne was at **LOOK/LISTEN**.

But at the same time, he did not know much about the Olympics. In fact, he did not even know when the next Olympics were scheduled nor anything about the process of how an Olympic city is chosen.

He began **STUDYING** and learned that the 1996 Games were the next on the list to be assigned a host city, and that to be considered, Atlanta had to be nominated first by the U.S. Olympic Committee (USOC) and then selected by the International Olympic Committee (IOC).

Armed with these basic facts, he **CONTINUED** his information search, discovering more details about the selection process and considering the advantages that the Olympics could offer Atlanta. Soon, this former University of Georgia football player was envisioning world-class athletes running, swimming, and biking in Atlanta, and he began **PLAYING** with the ideas of a Village for the athletes, Olympic venues scattered all over the state, and Atlanta turning into an international city.

After thinking his idea through, Payne made a firm decision. Atlanta definitely was the perfect city to host the 1996 Centennial Olympic Games, and he made a personal commitment to make that Olympic dream a reality.

Yet, as everyone knows, just having a great idea is not enough. If Payne were to bring the Olympics to Georgia, he needed more than just his commitment to his idea; he needed the help of others who shared his same level of commitment.

Unfortunately, the first people he approached with his idea were not at all interested. When he called on businesses or civic leaders, he met with indifference. After all, in the 1980s, Atlanta was not an international city, so why would an Atlanta leader bother to meet with Payne? (**NEGLECT**)

Some of the Atlanta leaders he talked with even complained that the city did not have the infrastructure or the know-how to host an Olympics and that such a venture would be cost prohibitive. "It is too late to get started on a project this big; bringing the Olympics to Atlanta involves too much work; we could never get the city ready in time for the 1996 Olympics," they told him. (**COMPLAIN**)

Others who heard about Payne's Olympic idea considered him a blowhard and his dream an embarrassment to the city. After all, they said, "Billy is just a real estate salesman with a frivolous Olympic scheme. Getting involved with him could be embarrassing." (**AVOID**)

A few of Atlanta's more prominent leaders like Atlanta Falcons owner Rankin Smith refused to even meet with Payne. To make matters even worse, both the Atlanta Metropolitan and the Georgia Chambers of Commerce turned down Payne's request for help and financial support. (**STOP**)

Outside of Atlanta, Payne faced even more challenges. People considered Payne's Olympic plan totally impossible, saying the South could never host the games because the region was poor, backward, unsophisticated, and technology limited. If that were not enough, they told Payne, no city had ever been awarded the Olympics on their first bid attempt. (**CHALLENGE**)

Undaunted by naysayers, Payne looked for support elsewhere. This time he went to longtime friends. He explained his idea to them, enabling them to come up the Decision Ladder with him, and soon they were just as committed to the Olympic dream as Payne. So committed were they that this group (known unofficially as the Atlanta Nine) provided much of the initial financing needed to fund the U.S. Olympic Committee (USOC) bid to be selected as the U.S. entry for the 1996 Olympic Games.

As momentum for his idea began building, Payne met with former Atlanta Mayor and U.N. Ambassador Andrew Young, and Payne convinced Young that the Olympic Dream for Atlanta would work. Ambassador Young proved to be a secret weapon for Payne and his newly formed Atlanta Olympic Committee (AOC). Andrew Young's networking, glittering Southern-style parties, Atlanta's Southern hospitality, and the spectacular Atlanta-hosted events won the U.S. Olympic team over. Atlanta was named the U.S. nominee for the 1996 Olympics.

Even though Atlanta was now the U.S. nominee, Payne and the Atlanta Olympic Committee had little money to go after the international bid. First, Payne and the AOC looked at all the options and possibilities open to them for their bid plans.

Then, Payne went back to the city's financial leaders and to the Atlanta Metro Area Chamber of Commerce, and this time they were open to his visit, listened to his proposal, and looked at his request for funding. (**LOOK/LISTEN**)

The Chamber granted Payne his funding and helped him gain millions more from the Atlanta business community. Now funded, Payne and the AOC began researching and planning their bid, learning as much as they could about the other competing cities and the Olympic committee members, and searching for a unique way to present Atlanta to the International Committee. (**STUDY**)

Continuing on his quest to showcase Atlanta, Payne asked the scientists at the Georgia Institute of Technology to create a dynamic presentation that would show off Atlanta's technology expertise. Georgia Tech's president rounded up more than 40 computer scientists to create an interactive showstopper with a virtual reality view of the Olympics in Atlanta. (**CONTINUE**)

The seven-foot tall, three-screen video offered a lifelike view of Atlanta, and by using its track ball and touch screen, IOC members could play with the system, virtually fly over the city, zoom in on buildings, walk through the Olympic Village, dive off a diving board, run down a track, and live the Olympics experience. (**PLAY**)

Just three years after Billy Payne started on his Olympic journey, IOC Chairman Juan Samaranch awarded the 1996 Centennial Olympic Games to Atlanta. The City of Atlanta achieved a success that no other American city had because Billy Payne had committed to an idea and led others to that same level of commitment by **RAISING** himself and making it easy for others to follow.

A more personal example of **RAISING** in action is this book. While PAR has been in business for more than 25 years, we were not always **COMMITTED** to writing a book about leadership. In fact, quite a few years went by before we reached a level of confidence that permitted us to actually **COMMIT** to writing *Cracking the Code*.

Early on, we were indifferent (**NEGLECT**) to the initial requests we had from clients who encouraged us to write a book that would reinforce our training programs. At that point, because we were a young company, the number of requests for a book was relatively small and just did not generate any interest on our part. Besides, we told ourselves, writing a book would take time, was hard work, involved long hours, and was something none of us had ever done. (**COMPLAIN**)

But the requests from our clients for a PAR book increased year after year. Yet, we were still apprehensive about putting our concepts in a book. Primarily, we were concerned that unscrupulous individuals would steal our concepts to use as their own. We saw this happen with Stephen Covey's *The Seven Habits of Highly Effective People* when a few consultants used entire sections of the book without attribution or claimed the material as their own (**AVOID**). Yet, that objection disappeared when someone pointed out that more than 500,000 people who trained in our programs already had our proprietary materials and, in most cases, they had respected our intellectual property.

Several times we **STOPPED** our book project before we actually started writing. One time, as we were planning the book's content, we found we were focusing on the shortcomings of other leadership programs, instead of the positive aspects of the PAR approach. So we stopped. Another time we stopped when we realized we had concentrated on the philosophy behind PAR instead of focusing on the actual skill set.

(For most people, **STOP** is the most difficult position on the Decision Ladder. Similar to the process used in tempering steel, a **STOP** will either make your idea stronger or make it brittle and break. In our case, each **STOP** we encountered played a major role in making our ultimate commitment that much stronger.)

Like all authors, we also faced the daunting **CHALLENGE** of getting our book published. To begin with, our book would have to compete with tens of thousands of other manuscripts just to get the attention of a literary agent and publisher.

On top of that, our **CHALLENGE** was even more difficult because *Cracking the Code* is about leadership, and leadership is the second most written about word in the English language. Yet, we opted to accept these **CHALLENGES** because they were so similar to the ones we faced over the past 25 years building our successful training and development organization.

Ultimately, we reached **LOOK/LISTEN** by removing all the negatives associated with the decision to write this book. As we pointed out earlier in this chapter, you cannot inspire others any higher than you are on the Decision Ladder. Therefore, we had to reach **COMMITMENT** to writing our book and remain at **COMMITMENT** throughout the entire process so that we could make reaching that same level of **COMMITMENT** easier for you and all who read this book.

Writing this book is actually a result of years of **STUDY** and a thorough analysis of facts. After **STUDYING** multitudes of leadership books over the past two decades, the one clear discovery we made is that no single book exists that illustrates the interpersonal skills of leadership for people to use in their everyday business or personal lives.

We also discovered that some of the more popular leadership books have generated training programs as a direct result of the books' success. Yet, readers of those books often reach an intellectual understanding of the content but are unable to implement what they read without a follow-up training program. Unfortunately, the follow-up training just gives them a deeper understanding of the leadership concepts. On the other hand, we have been creating real skill through our training programs for 30 years.

So, we **CONTINUED** our research and realized that almost every leadership book we studied had one thing in common. Somewhere in the book, the author would stress the importance of being a good listener and talk about the need to listen with empathy. Yet, not one of those books tells HOW to listen. Our book, we decided, would be different.

We **CONTINUED** moving forward, reviewing even more books. Ultimately, after much research and gathering materials, conducting brainstorming sessions, and consulting with our clients, we determined that the public needed a different kind of leadership book. Readers needed a book that would focus on the HOW: How to listen, how to listen with empathy and, more importantly, how to effectively lead.

With this in mind, we **CONTINUED** delving into the project and working on possible outlines and book guidelines.

Then, thinking about how the book would impact the people who read it, we began imagining the many careers and lives that our book could positively impact. We even began to **PLAY** with different titles for the book, ideas for the cover, and thoughts of making the business best-seller list.

So, we reached **COMMIT** after realizing the difference our book would make in so many business and personal lives. We became convinced and all agreed to **COMMIT** our time and effort to describing something about which we are truly passionate.

How does this story of our writing this book and those of Billy Payne's Olympic struggles and the Ford Mustang translate to you? Ask yourself: Would your business life be more successful if you were better at influencing your associates, your management, your team, or your customers? Would your personal life be more fulfilling if you were more effective at influencing and be more willingly influenced by your family, your friends, your neighbors, your church members, and others around you?

Leadership, as you now know, is a defined skill. See if you can put what you have learned so far into action. Think of an idea, either personal or business, that will obtain an outcome that you are committed to.

Maybe you have decided to take an extra course at the local college or you want to ask your manager for additional funding for a project. Whatever your idea is, remember what you want most is the result or the goal.

First, take yourself to **LOOK/LISTEN** on the Decision Ladder. What did you look at or consider? Next, go to **STUDY**. What are the details of your idea or how would your idea work? What would it do?

Now, **RAISE** yourself to **CONTINUE** and think about the advantages of your idea and how it could work even better than what is already being done. Then, finally, picture the results and **PLAY** with the thought of having your idea implemented. What would that look like?

Now, what can you **COMMIT** to today?

Try the same process again, but this time take a potential follower through the same progression up the Decision Ladder, and remember to constantly monitor your follower's attitudes and actions. Is your follower moving up with you? If so, keep **RAISING** yourself up the Decision Ladder to the biggest decision your follower can handle today.

If, however, your follower is not moving up the Ladder with you, then you will have some resistance to manage and that, by the way, is the subject of our next chapter.

Your ability to lead and influence others will not get you everything you want, but you will want everything you get. Instead of your success being in someone else's control, you can control your success. The only question now is what will you do with your ability to influence others and gain wholehearted followers for a given course of action?

Chapter 8

Headwinds and Thunderstorms:
Managing Resistance

"How do I overcome objections? How do I handle a 'No'? How do I deal with difficult people?"

At the beginning of our PAR training sessions, when we ask participants what they would like to achieve from their training, these by far are the most popular responses we hear. No matter what the focus of our training – whether leadership, management, teamwork, coaching, supervision, customer service, or sales skills – participants want to know how they can overcome objections and work with difficult people.

Most people seem programmed to think that if they can conquer or minimize a negative point of view that someone may have or get that person to drop his objections, they will achieve their goals. In other words, the common belief seems to be, *"If I prove my point, will you drop your objection?"*

Great leaders and statesmen know this is simply not the case. They realize that the *reasons* for objecting are infinite and that people use logic to justify their feelings.

Describing the futility of logic alone to resolve differences, Dean Rusk, Secretary of State under President John F. Kennedy, once said, "To me, the silliest argument in the world is, 'If you only knew what I know, you'd agree with me.'"

So, how do you handle objections? One way is to meet resistance with resistance, but in this case, the winner does not get a follower. The winner gets a loser who has surrendered for the time being and a loser who remembers the loss forever. Generally, when you meet resistance with resistance, you end up with compliance or, even worse, surrender. The reality is that if you use resistance, you may actually prove your point of view and win the argument, but you hardly ever receive wholehearted commitment and buy-in.

Given that the objective of leadership is to *"gain a wholehearted follower to a given course of action,"* you need to create a new mindset about resistance or objections and let go of any misconception you may have about handling resistance.

For many people, letting go of these misconceptions or flawed beliefs is tough. One of the most common flawed beliefs that people seem to have regarding resistance is that effective leaders can avoid resistance. This is simply not true.

What is true is that effective leaders are able to anticipate potential areas of resistance by knowing their potential followers quite well. Leaders deal with objections by precluding those objections in the way they present their ideas. However, because leaders are not all-knowing, they regularly encounter negative points of view throughout conversations.

By now, after reading the previous chapters, you know that effective leaders read their followers' heads and hearts (Chapters 1 & 2); prove they take other points of view seriously (Chapter 4); separate the person from the problem, i.e. triangulate the issue (Chapters 4 & 6); uncover key facts (Chapter 5), and position their ideas so they make sense to others (Chapter 6).

From the very start of our book, we have been showing you how to deal with objections and resistance. Any time a follower goes below Neutral, you have an objection or resistance that needs to be addressed.

To manage that resistance, you **PROBE**, recognize where that person is on the Decision Ladder, acknowledge that position, and ask more questions if necessary to truly understand the issue as the other person sees it. Then using the appropriate logic path dictated by the Decision Ladder, you **ALIGN** with the person's point of view to keep the conversation alive and productive.

As you do this, you remember that, in most cases, the other person is not objecting to the goal but objecting to your strategy for achieving that goal, which means you can still **ALIGN** by providing additional information or modifying your strategy.

So, in some respects, you already know how to manage resistance. Next, we come to a second flawed belief, which is that resistance needs to be overcome or objections need to be handled. Now, we do not know about you, but, personally, we hate the thought of someone *handling* us when we may object to something. Besides that, the word *overcome* implies having a winner and a loser, and no one we know of, inside or outside an organization, wants to be in a win-lose contest. Only your followers can change their minds, so do you want to help your followers or make them wrong?

Instead of overcoming or handling, start thinking about objections as issues to be answered and resistance as a concern to be managed. Think of an objection as your potential follower saying, *"I can't catch up to you at CONFIDENCE because of this issue or problem."* It only makes sense for you to **PROBE** by asking your followers to tell you more about that issue. After all, you want whole hearted buy-in to your approach. For that to happen, your potential followers must co-own your idea along with you.

While *handling* or *overcoming* negative views may win an argument for now, it never yields co-ownership. Instead, you end up with broken agreements and/or lack of goodwill, which are never acceptable outcomes for an effective leader.

The third flawed belief regarding resistance is one that we usually encounter when a client begins to see **P**ROBE-**A**LIGN-**R**AISE as some kind of a magical skill that eliminates all resistance. Just between you and us, we wish it were that simple because life would be so much easier.

However, we live in the real world where the people you deal with seem to have hundreds of ways to object, and that resistance is often the most difficult or the hardest to anticipate. This chapter is designed to show you how to use **P**ROBE-**A**LIGN-**R**AISE, even in the most difficult circumstances, to help you answer that resistance.

Over the years, with help from our clients and our own experiences, we developed a rogues' gallery of the most difficult types of resistance. See if you have ever encountered one of these rogues or if their behaviors sound familiar.

The Boy Scout

This potential follower is always prepared with a litany of reasons why your idea will never work. The Boy Scout utters such phrases as, "Yes, but have you thought about..." or "That may resolve that issue but what about...." Over time, the Boy Scout typically starts to get a reputation for always being negative and, therefore, may want to appear in a more favorable light. So, be prepared to hear the Boy Scout's same laundry list of objections, only now disguised as suggestions to help you make your idea better... "It looks like a reasonable idea, but let me play devil's advocate for a moment...."

The best strategy for dealing with a follower like the Boy Scout is acknowledging and NIQCL. At the first sign of resistance, acknowledge the Scout's point and ask, "What else?" Continue doing this until all the potential points of resistance are expressed. Once you finish with "N," move to "I" and rank the Boy Scout's resistance points in order of importance.

Based on our experience, you will see a significant reduction in the overall number of objections simply by bringing them to light, acknowledging and prioritizing them. With the remaining negative points, use "Q" to quantify or further reduce the list and then go to "C" consequences to cull out the remainder, so you are left with just one or two real objections to resolve.

As the leader, you reduce your agenda of objections by acknowledging and using NIQCL. Your potential followers feel good because you have taken them seriously, so they will now take your idea seriously and help solve the remaining objections.

The Bully

The Bully can be highly emotional, raise his voice, bang on a conference table, and use a variety of other intimidating physical actions to make his point. Occasionally, the Bully is a she, and her intimidation may be tears. Psychologists are probably better equipped than we are to explain why some people behave this way. The question for you is what can you do to manage this kind of behavior? The answer is simply one word: Confidence.

The key to managing the Bully is to remain confident in the face of the Bully's aggressive tactics. Your acknowledgements should be confined to continual eye contact, an occasional nod of the head, brief responses like, "Okay," "Got It," "Mmm," or the offer of a tissue. All the time, let the Bully rage on.

When he/she winds down (and the Bully will eventually), then it is appropriate to acknowledge what you heard, putting in suitable energy to let the Bully know you take him/her seriously and ask if he/she has any other concerns. The quicker the Bully realizes that he/she cannot intimidate you, the quicker the Bully will stop behaving like a corporate bully and return to normal accepted business behavior.

The Poker Player

The tactics of the Poker Player are the exact opposite of the Bully. With the Poker Player, you see little verbal communication, and body language is solid Neutral and stays there. The Poker Player could love your idea or hate your idea; you just do not know.

With this type of personality, you need to draw the individual out. The most skillful way to do this is reading what you are seeing and hearing and then asking the right questions, such as, *"You haven't said much. What do you think so far?"*

If the Poker Player initially gives you short answers, for example, "It looks good so far," you need to clarify what that means with follow-up questions. Ask, *"What part looks good to you?"* or *"I know when I say something looks good so far that I am pretty positive. However, I do not want to get in trouble by making an assumption here. So, can you help me? How do you see it?"*

You may not get elaborate responses or significant body language from the Poker Player. This means you must pay close attention to the little communication you receive, putting a high value on your listening and observation skills, so that you can properly **ALIGN**.

The Roller Coaster

Because more complex decisions often have multiple points of view, you may encounter the Roller Coaster or that person whose responses go up and down during a conversation. With the Roller Coaster, the key is to display patience while being persistent. You need to be persistent about achieving your goals or objectives but patient in helping Roller Coasters through their ups and downs.

For example, take the complex decision of purchasing a new home. Roller Coaster-prospective homebuyers may love the school district but hate the chain-link fence in the backyard. They may feel the house is priced right, but the homeowner's association fees and property taxes may strain the budget. They may love the three-car garage but hate the hour's commute to work. In this home-buying situation, NIQCL can help the real estate agent or home seller determine which negative points are deal breakers and which ones the Roller Coaster potential buyers will accept.

The Einstein

Occasionally, you will encounter an Einstein, a person with a point of resistance that is so complex, so difficult, that you have absolutely no idea how to approach that resistance. In this situation, we recommend that you acknowledge the dilemma you face and ask the Einstein for potential solutions. If both of you are stumped, then you might want to apply these ten tests derived from the Decision Ladder and determine:

What part of the problem can be neglected for now?

What part needs some outside help?

What part can be avoided for now or permanently?

What part can we stop now?

What part can we challenge?

What part can be looked at leisurely for now?

What part needs more study or information?

What part can be continued as is?

What ideas can be played with right now?

What part can be accepted and committed to right now?

Working with these ten questions will help you realize two important points. First, you do not need to be the one with all the answers. Sometimes, the person closest to the problem has the solution or can provide the key to finding the solution. Second, when complex issues are broken down into more manageable parts, solutions tend to be discovered easier and quicker.

Consider the challenge President Kennedy made to America's scientific community in 1961 when he announced that the United States would place a man on the moon before the end of the decade. If the entire scientific community had focused on the overall mission, the United States probably would still be trying to figure out the solution. Instead, a group of engineers tackled propulsion, others looked at navigation, another group at guidance, others at the Lunar Lander, some at astronaut selection and training, and so forth. By breaking down the most complex challenge of that generation into manageable parts, America successfully met Kennedy's challenge.

The Wild Bunch

Sometimes leadership feels very much like trying to herd a bunch of cats. Because not all leadership moments take place in one-on-one conversations, leaders often must herd or manage a wild bunch of followers, with multiple attitudes, all in the same conversation.

To show you how an effective leader should deal with the Wild Bunch, let us examine a typical business scenario. Assume you are a product manager with a new product developed in R&D. You believe the product is ready to launch, and now you must make your case to the Director of Sales & Marketing, the Vice President of Operations, the Vice President of Finance, the R&D Manager, and the General Counsel.

Obviously, because each department head potentially has a different point of view, having one-on-one conversations would be much easier for you than dealing with several decision makers all at the same time, all in the same meeting, and with dynamics all over the place. But, more often than not, you will face a situation where one-on-ones are not possible, and you must make your case before a group.

Your probing skills are especially important when managing resistance with a group. Every individual in your meeting is important to the outcome, or they would not be there. So, with this group, and with most groups, rule number one is to treat everyone as an equal regardless of business title or responsibility.

During your meeting, you may be able to get a commitment from the highest-ranking member of the group, but after you leave, the others in the group will spend their time trying to undo that decision. Even if the decision stands up under pressure, what kind of execution do you think you are going to get from those who are not committed to the product?

In order to prepare for your group meeting, let us assume that you met one-on-one with each participant. From those individual meetings, you learn that:

The Director of Sales & Marketing loves the product as is and is pushing to fast track the launch into the marketplace within the next 90 days.

The Vice President of Operations likes the idea but is adamant about getting accurate forecasts from the sales department so that inventory levels do not exceed a thirty-day supply, so she can plan long production runs to reduce manufacturing costs.

The Vice President of Finance opposes a fast-track launch because the company has heavy inventory quantities of a similar product that will have to be closed out at a loss if the new launch cannibalizes the sales of the existing product.

The R&D Manager, uncomfortable with some of the stated benefits of the new product, would like another six months of testing to verify performance.

The General Counsel, who just finished negotiating a product-liability lawsuit on a previous launch, complains about opening another can of worms.

Even though you enter your group meeting knowing how each department head stands, you also realize that your one-on-one meetings were last week, and a number of your decision makers have histories of changing their minds overnight, let alone after a week's passage of time.

Your plan is to open the meeting with your Decision Goal and then deal with the lowest attitude first (the General Counsel's **COMPLAIN**) and work your way up the Decision Ladder (R&D **AVOID**, Finance **STOP**, and Operations **CHALLENGE**) until the entire group is at Neutral. At this point, you plan to roll out your recommended launch strategy (**STUDY**), field their questions (**CONTINUE**), help them imagine the market's reaction and the impact on their annual bonuses and profit sharing (**PLAY**), and end with a strong closing that engages them all as co-owners of their parts in making the launch successful (**COMMIT**).

This is the exact strategy we would recommend. Unfortunately, this meeting takes place in the real world, which means, to paraphrase famed poet Robert Burns, "The best made plans of mice and men often go awry."

In this meeting scenario, shortly after you present your Decision Goal, the R&D Manager reveals the product has failed a performance test criteria and wants to delay the launch. Just by looking at the group's reactions, you know that the R&D Manager's announcement has changed everyone's attitude, but you are not sure what their new attitudes are or what their positions are on the Decision Ladder.

Rarely will a group sit and allow you to poll them one at a time to determine their attitudes. So, instead of probing each individual, **PROBE** the entire group together. When someone expresses a negative position, acknowledge it. (*"It sounds like there may be a performance problem. Tell us more about it."*) Then ask the others how they see the issue. (*"Is that aspect of performance a problem for the rest of you?"*)

By probing and acknowledging, you keep the group together and participating. This also allows you to pull into the discussion those who are not participating. Probing the group as a whole keeps you from feeling like a ping-pong ball being smashed between the members of the group.

Keep in mind you may have a Boy Scout, a Bully, a Poker Player, a Roller Coaster, or even an Einstein participating in any meeting. The one common denominator in dealing with all these varied types is maintaining your confidence while **PROBING**, acknowledging and using NIQCL questions. You must become the Master of the PAR Skills, which will only add to your confidence.

On the other hand, high interest participants (**CONTINUE**) can be just as damaging to the entire group because they ask question after question and do not let anyone else talk. Undoubtedly, you have been in meetings and seen eyes roll when one person tries to positively dominate the meeting for one reason or another.

If this happens in your meeting, acknowledge that there are a lot of questions and that you want to make sure you answer all of them, and then ask how the others in the meeting see the situation.

Occasionally, you will find yourself with people who have entirely different agendas. In those cases, a separate meeting with each individual works better than trying to achieve your goal in a single group setting. For instance, if you are advocating new technology, the technical experts within your organization will have different agendas than the end-users. By holding a separate meeting with each group, you keep everyone engaged and focused. You may even find you will spend less total time having two focused meetings rather than one all-over-the-place meeting.

Similarly, you may find yourself in a group situation where one person has an issue that needs attention but does not impact anyone else. In this instance, acknowledge the issue, park it for the group meeting, and set up a one-on-one meeting with the person to resolve the issue.

When dealing with groups, here are five important strategic points to know. First, position yourself where you have a reasonable line of sight to everyone at the meeting and maintain eye contact with all participants. Doing so helps keep the meeting on track and people engaged. For instance, if you respond to a person on a specific issue, and you only focus on that person, you run the risk of losing the others in the audience. So, be in a position that allows you to easily make eye contact with everyone.

The second point to remember is to slow down your rate of speech when talking to a group of people. The natural tendency is to speed up when dealing with multiple people, so by making an effort to slow your speech down, you will reach a happy medium.

Third, know that everyone has a limit to the size group he or she can effectively lead in an interactive discussion. Your maximum will depend on your skill level, but for even the most skilled people, the maximum is approximately ten participants. Groups of over ten are best managed with a one-way presentation followed by a Q & A session.

Fourth, everyone in the group is important to the outcome and possible implementation of your idea. Remember that when you make a presentation or sell your idea. More importantly, do not make the mistake that so many people do and direct your conversation to the most senior people present, assuming they are the only decision makers. Unfortunately, after such a conversation, the others present in the meeting may try to un-sell your idea or make implementation a nightmare. The best strategy is to treat everyone in the meeting as equals.

Our fifth and last point, and perhaps the most important one, is that when you answer objections or manage resistance, your goal is to get a decision, not win an argument. Sometimes the decision will be *"No,"* and all the leadership skills in the world will not change that. However, if you know the reason for the *"No,"* then that *"No"* could be viewed as *"No, for now,"* and you have permission to do more work on the idea and re-present it when you have a better idea.

To help you sharpen your skills at managing resistance, we want you to try two exercises we use in our classes. The first one is to look over a list of the five most common objections people encounter.

Carefully review each objection and then take your best guess at identifying where the point of view for that objection would be on the Decision Ladder. (*As you do this, remember that without the music of a conversation, these objections are just words on paper.*)

Now, on a sheet of paper, write down the Decision Ladder level and how you would respond to each of these objections.

A. "That won't work."

B. "No point in covering that. I don't use it, and I don't think anyone else does either."

C. "I worry that we are going to spend all this money and not see any significant improvement."

D. "You have to show me proof that restructuring will have the desired results."

E. "I have two large projects and no spare time to get involved with another initiative."

When you finish responding to all five objections, compare your answers with our list of possible strategies found on the next few pages.

Answers

A.   "That won't work."

We started you out with a tough one because without conversational music, this objection could reasonably be at **COMPLAIN**, **STOP,** or **CHALLENGE**.

If you acknowledged **STOP**, then the appropriate strategy would be to follow the objection with a question, i.e. *"What's wrong?"* to determine the reason for the **STOP**.

If you acknowledged **CHALLENGE**, then an appropriate strategy would be to offer some type of proof. If you do not know what kind of proof would be acceptable, then you could ask what kind of information would be required to justify it.

If you acknowledged **COMPLAIN**, then your appropriate strategy would be to ask questions regarding the difficulty and then determine how you might help.

B.   "No point in covering that. I don't use it, and I don't think anyone else does either."

You should have acknowledged **NEGLECT**, and then the strategy could be either to find out what this person does use or thank him for his time and move on. You may even have a third option, which would be to check with the others to verify whether or not they use it.

C.   "I worry that we are going to spend all this money and not see any significant improvement."

Again, without the music, determining the Decision Ladder level may be unclear, but we intended it to be **AVOID**. Handle this response by acknowledging **AVOID**, ask what risks the person sees, and then present a strategy that minimizes and/or eliminates the perceived risks.

D.   "You have to show me proof that restructuring will have the desired results."

This statement is clearly **CHALLENGE**. Acknowledge the **CHALLENGE**, ask what kind of proof the person needs for justification, and then offer proof that the restructuring will deliver the desired results.

E.   "I have two large projects and no spare time to get involved with another initiative."

Acknowledge **COMPLAIN**, ask about the other projects the person is handling, and then offer some type of help, i.e. reprioritize projects, temporary assistance, etc.

After you have practiced with these artificial objections, we want you to try a second exercise. This one involves real work. First, identify an area in your company or business where people show chronic resistance or reluctance to implementing a given process, plan, or change. Now follow Steps 1-6 below:

1.   Use every level on the Decision Ladder to think through this process, plan, or change. With the levels on the bottom half, think about the potential reasons that would cause someone's resistance. On the top half, think through the positive benefits of this new process, plan, or change.

2.   Admit to yourself that you only have a 10% chance of being correct on either side of the Decision Ladder.

3.   Now, ask the people directly how they see the situation. Use your probing skills to identify their individual points of view, fully acknowledge their views, and use NIQCL if you need to do any in-depth probing.

4.   Take some time to think through what you have heard and then go back to each individual with a potential solution for each objection given. This may not solve every problem, but see if the other people are not higher on the Decision Ladder than you originally found them.

5.   Assess each encounter by asking yourself:

Were they listened to and taken seriously before?

Has anyone ever aligned with them in a way that made sense to them?

What did the NIQCL questions tell you?

Were the solutions obvious to you after probing and aligning?

6.   Take a leadership position on the issue based on everything you learned in Steps 1-5. Then determine the biggest decision that each person can make right now. If you moved them higher than they were in Step 4, you have a win. If everyone reaches **COMMITMENT**, you have a BIG win.

In either case, whether you have a win or a big win, congratulations. You successfully managed resistance and answered objections in a real work situation. You can **P**ROBE-**A**LIGN-**R**AISE in difficult situations. You are well on your way to cracking the leadership code and positively impacting your business career and your personal life.

All that remains are some finishing touches that we outline in the next chapters.

Chapter 9

Reaching the Finish Line

There comes a time when all your hard work and preparation come together, and the time is right to go for closure! This is the moment you go for commitment.

In business, whenever people interact, they make decisions: a decision to talk, a decision to listen, a decision to act on a recommendation.

Ideally, as a leader, you want your followers to make decisions that are both well informed and high on the Decision Ladder. The reason for this is twofold. First, the higher your followers are on the Decision Ladder, when they reach a final decision, the more effort and quality they will put into carrying through that decision.

At **COMMIT**, your follower, or the Decider, owns the result and outcome just as much as you. At the highest level on the Decision Ladder, the Decider is committed to seeing the decision through, definitely more than someone who only thinks (**STUDY**) your idea may be good, more than the person who expresses interest (**CONTINUE**) in the idea, and more than the follower who may be excited (**PLAY**) by the idea.

Second, agreements can come from any level on the Decision Ladder, but commitments only come at the top. This means the extra time needed to gain a commitment, instead of an agreement, is definitely worth your effort. When your followers are negative towards your idea, but agree with the idea anyway, they are either surrendering or complying. Neither is acceptable if you seek *willing* followers.

In most cases, when surrender or compliance from followers occurred, the leader used positional or economic power to achieve that result. This type of command leadership, while occasionally acceptable, is never appropriate when you seek a co-owner of your idea.

Oftentimes, people may say they are committed to an idea, but then they fail to follow through. When this happens, the leader, more often than not, has misread his followers and confused a high level of agreement with commitment.

Agreement and commitment are not the same. You can gain agreement from people at **LOOK/LISTEN** all the way up the Decision Ladder to **PLAY**. However, agreement at any of these levels is simply based on good intentions at that moment in time and, as such, is subject to change with the passage of time or an additional conversation.

Commitments are decisions that people willingly reach from confidence. In other words, when people are committed, they believe in their decisions and own them. Their decisions are promises, convictions, and definitely much more than agreements. The highest quality and quantity of results occur when someone really becomes a customer or co-owner of an idea and acts on that idea without reservation.

In any organization, agreements can come from neutral or any positive level up to **PLAY** on the Decision Ladder. However, with commitment, the will to take action, and own that action, comes from the very top. Even **PLAY** on the Decision Ladder is close, but it is not closed. **PLAY** represents good intentions that can be eroded with the first problem or issue. How often have you talked about how great a party or event would be, but you did not attend?

Or conversely, have you had people tell you your idea was fantastic, but they failed to act on it? Unfortunately, this happens all too often in business, and results are rarely what you wish for. If you are a manager who is constantly following up with your people to make sure they are following through, you do not have their commitment.

A good example of **PLAY** being misinterpreted as **COMMIT** occurred with one of our clients engaged in market research for a new product introduction. Their new product would answer many complaints doctors and their clients had about compliance issues with existing products. The market research results were regularly sprinkled with doctor/client comments such as "It's about time," "This will make my life so much easier," "That's a brilliant idea," etc. These glowing responses convinced many at our client's company that a large and viable market existed for the potential new product.

Fortunately, an astute marketing manager, realizing that most of the research comments were coming from **PLAY**, commissioned a follow-up study with those respondents. This time, researchers asked the doctors if they would prescribe the product and asked their clients if they would consider using the product. Responses varied, ranging from **AVOID** to **CONTINUE** with only a few at **COMMIT**. Misreading enthusiasm from **COMMITMENT** could have cost our client millions of dollars. This is why remembering that true commitments only come from confidence is so important.

The purpose of this chapter is to help you gain commitments instead of just getting agreements that may or may not stick. The three critical components to making this happen are to know:

1. When to go for closure and commitment

2. How to get commitments and bring closure

3. How to handle stalls or indecisions

Let us start with the first component — *When to go for closure.* You go for closure when the Decision Maker is as high on the Decision Ladder as he or she is likely to get to today. Doing this has several different implications. First and foremost is that the biggest decision your follower can handle today may not be a positive decision.

For instance, your follower may need some proof (**CHALLENGE**) that you may not have right then. In this case, you would want to close the conversation for today at **CHALLENGE** and reconvene at a later date when you have the proof. One way to close such a conversation would be to say, "Sounds like more proof is needed before we can move forward. Let me do some homework, and let's reconvene next Monday to review my findings."

Trying to close for a positive decision when your Decider is below neutral is premature and too fast. In essence, you are trying to jump from **PROBE** straight to **RAISE** without first **ALIGNING**. This is where *"Yes, but"* originates. By saying, *"Yes, but,"* you are, in essence, telling the Decider, *"You are being illogical."* Would you react positively to someone who says that to you? Probably not!

The old-school way to go for the close in business is to say, *"If I can show you a way, would you do business?"* But this closing statement really means, *"If I can prove my point, will you drop all of yours?"* This approach, which seldom works, is a direct result of trying to close for a positive response at negative levels of the Decision Ladder.

Any time your follower is above neutral, you are closing for positive commitment. Even though your ultimate goal is to close for a commitment to action and corresponding results, that may not always be possible today. Sometimes the biggest decision you can get today is a commitment to more thought (**STUDY**). Or maybe the biggest decision is a commitment to more discussion (**CONTINUE**) or even a commitment to more imagining the future (**PLAY**). What you want is a *"Yes"* and a well-informed decision, even though such a decision, at this moment in time, may not be the ultimate one of co-owning your idea.

However, no matter what the biggest decision is that your follower can make today, put closure to it with the understanding you need to continue to lead that conversation to your end goal, which is a commitment or co-ownership.

As you know, often in business, many little decisions occur before the final, ultimate decision. Obviously, not every business conversation ends in a commitment to action. So, closing often is a test of your patience and persistence. The important point to remember is that you close when the Decider has reached the highest point on the Decision Ladder he or she can reach in a conversation.

That brings us to the second critical component for gaining commitments – *How to close.* Or simply put, *How do you go from close to closed?* The answer to that question is – Confidently.

Almost every book on business negotiation, sales, or management suggests that you *ask* for the business. You *ask* for the commitment. Therein lies a problem. When you ask questions, such as *"Would you like to move ahead? Would you like to get started? Can we do business?,"* you communicate at the **STUDY** or **CONTINUE** levels on the Decision Ladder. The result is your follower aligns with you there and wants to talk more or ask more questions.

A far more effective approach is to take yourself to confidence and suggest the action by closing with a statement – *"I recommend we get started." "Let's do it." "I need your okay."* You take yourself to **COMMIT** on the Decision Ladder and see if the Decider will **ALIGN** with you at **COMMIT**. In other words, when you use statements that show your confidence, you are likely to receive confidence and action in return.

Most of the movement above **CONTINUE** on the Decision Ladder is a leap of faith. Facts, for the most part, diminish after **CONTINUE**. **PLAY** is an exercise of your imagination, and **COMMIT** is a complete exercise in confidence. Buying a house, buying a car, and getting married are all leaps of faith. More than likely, you took a leap of faith to take your current job, your last assignment, or your most recent promotion. Nothing in life is guaranteed. There may be warranties but not guarantees.

Considering that a move from **CONTINUE** to **PLAY** to **COMMIT** requires a leap of faith on the part of the Decider, to make that leap, the Decider needs to see your confidence in your idea, recommendation, or suggestion. So, if you ask, *"Do you want to make the move?,"* you are abdicating the decision, totally washing your hands of your idea, right in front of the Decider. More importantly, you fail to show confidence. No wonder, when people are placed in situations like this, they are likely to consider the idea all over again or even stall their decisions.

When you close a conversation with a strong confident statement, you show your own conviction. You show that it is your idea that you believe in, and that you are already confident. As a leader, you must be able to make the leap of faith first, which makes it easier for your follower to join you at confidence.

Think about all the leadership interactions you have had throughout your personal life and business life. Likely you did not ask your followers to join you. Instead, you drew a conclusion and suggested moving forward. You demonstrated your own confidence.

Here is a little test. Just for fun, ask yourself, which sounds more confident: The question, *"Would you dance with me?"* or the statement, *"Let's dance."* We suspect the statement will deliver many more dance partners than the question. Closing with a statement gets a commitment to action.

Often, people say they are committed to an idea but then fail to follow through on that commitment. As we pointed out earlier, this situation usually happens when a leader misreads his followers. But this also occurs when people are negative to an idea but are intimidated by their leader's title and surrender or comply. Closing with a call to action normally brings negative positions to the surface earlier and allows you, as the leader, to deal with the resistance sooner rather than later.

You may occasionally have a follower say, *"If I have to...."* Such a statement signals surrender and compliance, not commitment. With an attitude like this, your follower, at the first sign of trouble, will abandon ship and point the finger at someone else.

Obtaining real commitment, not simply surrender, compliance, or even agreement, is the key to having your followers' buy-in and ensuring their follow-through.

Sometimes, when you close with a statement, you will sense some indecision and that brings us to the third critical aspect of gaining commitment: *What to do in the face of stalls or indecision.* You have probably guessed the answer – more **P**ROBE-**A**LIGN-**R**AISE.

Stalls and/or indecision are signals that Deciders are having trouble reaching a conclusion. They need your help. So, you **PROBE** to recognize where they are on the Decision Ladder, acknowledge, and ask appropriate questions. You may even want to use the NIQCL questions from Chapter 4 to help diagnose the reasons for the stall or indecision.

Sometimes, the Deciders are not that communicative, and the reasons for their stalls or indecisions are unstated. Even though you have answered all their questions and everything seems in order, the Deciders are still undecided and unwilling to make a decision.

Because their objections or resistance are not stated, resolving their issues is all the more difficult. One approach that works and makes it safe for the Decider to talk is to admit that *"NO"* is a decision you are willing to accept, if the *"NO"* is confident and well informed.

To get the Decider to open up about his or her reservations, you could say something as simple as, *"If this doesn't give you the confidence you need to move ahead, then you shouldn't,"* and then ask about the person's reservations. Or you could say, *"Is there something that is keeping you from reaching confidence in this approach?"*

PROBING this way often gives your followers the permission and security they need, so they can tell you their concerns. Just be careful not to rush to solve the problem. **PROBE** with patience. Doing so allows you to **ALIGN** in a manner that is comfortable with indecisive followers.

On the other hand, sometimes in business, a **NO** decision is valid. When the Decider is confident and well informed, you must accept **NO** with grace and confidence. For instance, if someone accepts a well-informed and committed *"No"* from you and thanks you for the opportunity, would you not be more willing to listen to a different approach, at a different time, to achieve a mutual goal? Of course you would, and most people feel the same way.

But what if you encounter the opposite approach? Someone keeps pushing, trying to talk, or even forcing you to decide **YES**. Would you be willing to take that person's calls or give him or her an appointment? Probably not! So, the issue becomes your ability to read another person to know when a *"No"* is well informed and committed.

Try this quick exercise to help you read a **NO**. Say **NO** out loud at each level on the Decision Ladder, saying:

1. *"No"* as if you are indifferent. (**NEGLECT**)

2. *"No"* as if you are troubled. (**COMPLAIN**)

3. *"No"* as if you see risks. (**AVOID**)

4. *"No"* as if you are opposed. (**STOP**)

5. *"No"* as if you are skeptical. (**CHALLENGE**)

6. *"No"* as if you are neutral. (**LOOK/LISTEN**)

7. *"No"* as if you are reserved. (**STUDY**)

8. *"No"* as if you are still interested. (**CONTINUE**)

9. *"No"* as if you are still enthused. (**PLAY**)

10. Now say *"No"* from confidence. (**COMMIT**)

You can hear the difference, which is how you know whether to accept the **NO** or keep communicating and continuing to **P**ROBE-**A**LIGN-**R**AISE.

Going for a decision is the hallmark skill of leadership. You are the Decision Getter and your follower is the Decision Maker. If you want buy-in, commitment, and co-ownership, you **P**ROBE-**A**LIGN-**R**AISE for the biggest decision the Decision Maker can make at that moment in time.

Going for a decision with confidence should not be viewed as the last opportunity to convince your audience, but as the first opportunity to show your follower you are convinced.

Now that you know when and how to go for the close, it is your turn to try going for the close and closing. Practice your closing with these four assignments:

1. Find a practice partner and try closing a conversation with a question, such as *"So, do you want to move ahead?"* Watch your partner's reaction. Does he or she look away, seem to think the question over even for a brief moment, or actually go down the Decision Ladder?

Now, repeat the same exercise, but instead of a question, close the conversation with a suggested action, using a statement such as *"Let's get started."* Watch the other person's reaction. Does he or she join you in the action, make eye contact, or act without reservation?

2. Again, with your practice partner, see how far you can go with your confidence before he or she tells you that what you said sounded arrogant. Most of us under-power our closing because we are afraid of sounding arrogant. Find out where that line is for you; then dial back just a little. Then repeat it three or four times, so you can begin to build the muscle memory to replicate it at will.

3. The next time you are in a conversation with a customer, your project team, or your peers, when you sense they are high on the Decision Ladder, suggest an appropriate action to bring closure to your discussion. What happens? Do they join you in that action?

4. Take a few minutes to review the Decision Goals outlined in Chapter 3. As you do, keep in mind that leaders are confident and committed to their goals but flexible in regard to the strategies necessary to achieve those goals.

Knowing when and how to gain commitment as well as handling stalls or indecision are key to successful leadership and are the final pieces to mastering the PAR Skill Set.

As we said before, leadership is not some mysterious art form. Leadership is a concrete, definable, repeatable skill that leaders previously used instinctively. We encourage you to follow these PAR Skills, make them an integral part of your everyday life, and use them to help you reach your goals, build and nurture relations, and turn your dreams into reality. You can do this and succeed because you have cracked the elusive code to successful leadership.

Now that you have discovered the secret behind leadership and know the steps to being an effective leader, we have put together a series of business anecdotes, success stories, and other pointers in the next few chapters to help guide you on your road to successful leadership.

Section Five

PAR Leadership at Work

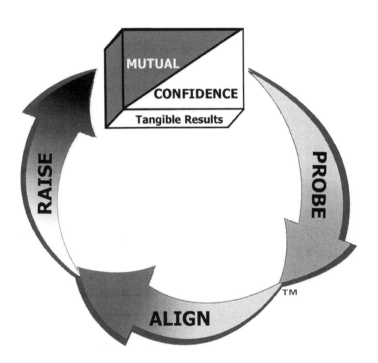

Chapter 10

PAR in Action

We included real-life examples in each chapter to show you how our PAR skills work. By seeing PAR in action, you are able to better verify the skills and how they apply to actual situations.

If you were to take a PAR training session, you would be able to quickly get the feel of using the PAR Skills because you would practice using real business ideas with real decision makers. You could test your ability while conducting real work.

But because you are reading the book and not in a training class right now, we want to simulate, as much as possible, those real-world experiences that our training participants have by providing you with additional examples of PAR leadership skills and the Decision Ladder at work. The scenarios found in this chapter will give you another chance to prove the PAR skills will work for you.

To start with, consider Winston Churchill, John Kennedy, Ronald Reagan, and Dr. Martin Luther King, Jr. These men, among the world's greatest leaders, initially stood alone at **COMMIT** to their goals. Like so many of great leadership icons, Churchill, Kennedy, Reagan, and Dr. King knew they needed to build a following for the goals they set forth.

When celebrated leaders give a speech before a large audience, they know they must somehow connect with and inspire a new point of view for many of their listeners. Statistics alone bear out the assumption that in an audience of thousands, a leader's potential followers are likely spread along all spectrums of the Decision Ladder with some at **NEGLECT**, **COMPLAIN**, **AVOID**, and others at **STOP** or **CHALLENGE**. True leaders intuitively know this. A leader's success depends on connecting first with those who are at these levels before inviting them to NEUTRAL and beyond.

Perfect examples of this instinctive ability on the part of distinguished leaders are found in many of the speeches that changed the face of the world as we know it. For instance, consider U.S. President Ronald Reagan and his *Tear Down This Wall* speech that historians consider to be the catalyst behind the dissolution of the former Soviet Union.

As you read the following excerpts from this June 12, 1987, address delivered at the foot of the symbolic Brandenburg Gate in Berlin, note how President Reagan builds his case up the Decision Ladder from **COMPLAIN** all the way to ultimate commitment.

"Behind me stands a wall that encircles the free sectors of this city, part of a vast system of barriers that divides the entire continent of Europe. From the Baltic, south, those barriers cut across Germany in a gash of barbed wire, concrete, dog runs, and guard towers." (**COMPLAIN**)

"Farther south, there may be no visible, no obvious wall. But there remain armed guards and checkpoints all the same – still a restriction on the right to travel, still an instrument to impose upon ordinary men and women the will of a totalitarian state." (**AVOID**)

"Yet, it is here in Berlin where the wall emerges most clearly; here, cutting across your city, where the news photo and the television screen have imprinted this brutal division of a continent upon the mind of the world. Standing before the Brandenburg Gate, every man is a German, separated from his fellow men. Every man is a Berliner, forced to look upon a scar." (**STOP**)

"Today I say: As long as the gate is closed, as long as this scar of a wall is permitted to stand, it is not the German question alone that remains open, but the question of freedom for all mankind." (**CHALLENGE**)

"Yet I do not come here to lament. For I find in Berlin a message of hope, even in the shadow of this wall, a message of triumph." (**LOOK/LISTEN**)

"In the Reichstag a few moments ago, I saw a display commemorating this 40th anniversary of the Marshall Plan. I was struck by the sign on a burnt-out, gutted structure that was being rebuilt. I understand that Berliners of my own generation can remember seeing signs like it dotted throughout the western sectors of the city.

"The sign read simply: 'The Marshall Plan is helping here to strengthen the free world.' A strong, free world in the West, that dream became real. Japan rose from ruin to become an economic giant. Italy, France, Belgium – virtually every nation in Western Europe saw political and economic rebirth; the European Community was founded." **(STUDY)**

"In West Germany and here in Berlin, there took place an economic miracle, the Wirtschaftswunder. Adenauer, Erhard, Reuter, and other leaders understood the practical importance of liberty – that just as truth can flourish only when the journalist is given freedom of speech, so prosperity can come about only when the farmer and businessman enjoy economic freedom. The German leaders reduced tariffs, expanded free trade, lowered taxes. From 1950 to 1960 alone, the standard of living in West Germany and Berlin doubled." **(CONTINUE)**

"Where four decades ago there was rubble, today in West Berlin there is the greatest industrial output of any city in Germany – busy office blocks, fine homes and apartments, proud avenues, and the spreading lawns of parkland. Where a city's culture seemed to have been destroyed, today there are two great universities, orchestras and an opera, countless theaters, and museums. Where there was want, today there's abundance – food, clothing, automobiles – the wonderful goods of the Ku'damm. From devastation, from utter ruin, you Berliners have, in freedom, rebuilt a city that once again ranks as one of the greatest on earth. The Soviets may have had other plans. But my friends, there were a few things the Soviets didn't count on – Berliner Herz, Berliner Humor, ja, und Berliner Schnauze. [Berliner heart, Berliner humor, yes, and a Berliner Schnauze.]" **(PLAY)**

"General Secretary Gorbachev, if you seek peace, if you seek prosperity for the Soviet Union and Eastern Europe, if you see liberation: Come here to this gate! Mr. Gorbachev, open this gate! Mr. Gorbachev, tear down this wall!" **(COMMIT)**

Just from this speech, you can see why President Reagan is called The Great Communicator. (You can read *Tear Down This Wall* in its entirety as well as other Reagan speeches at www.reaganfoundation.org.)

Another speech with worldwide impact and one that truly changed the face of America was delivered as part of a massive march on Washington, D.C., on August 28, 1963. Standing on the steps of the Lincoln Memorial, the Reverend Dr. Martin Luther King, Jr. provided a seminal moment in the Civil Rights Movement with his *I Have a Dream* speech.

You can find Dr. King's legendary speech at http://www.usconstitution.net/dream.html and as you read the words of this Civil Rights leader, consider these points:

What could be more *troubling* than 100 years after the signing of the Emancipation Proclamation that people of color were still not free?

What could be more *fearful* than a returned check marked insufficient funds?

What could be more *hostile* than refusing to believe our justice system was bankrupt?

What could be more *competitive* than to demand now is the time and not underestimate our determination?

As he spoke that day to the multitude before him and the millions watching the march on television, Dr. King answered these questions, skillfully using the bottom half of the Decision Ladder to articulate the dreadful conditions African-Americans faced in the America of 1963. From here, he next invited his audience to NEUTRAL to hear his nonviolent strategy for social change, and he sketched out his plan at **STUDY** and **CONTINUE**. Then he **PLAYED** with the possibilities through his dreams and ended at absolute **COMMIT** with that famous lyric of the old spiritual, *Free at Last.*

You can find similar examples of speeches by famous leaders who intuitively used the Decision Ladder to engage their audiences and help their listeners/followers reach **COMMIT**. Abraham Lincoln did it in his *Gettysburg Address* and so did Winston Churchill in his *We Shall Fight on the Beaches* speech before the House of Commons on June 4, 1940. President Kennedy's *We Choose to Go to the Moon* speech at Rice University, on September 12, 1962; Nelson Mandela's Inaugural Address on May 10, 1994; and President George W. Bush's Address to the Nation on September 11, 2001 are further examples of leaders inspiring their audiences with the Decision Ladder.

We encourage you to read these speeches, or any other famous speech, while holding the PAR Decision Ladder in your hand. As you read, note how the speaker takes his audience up the Decision Ladder.

All the speeches mentioned here, and most of the world's legendary speeches, are available today in audio format. We recommend that you listen to speeches too. Listen not just to the words or to what the speakers are saying, but also listen to the music or how the speakers say their words. Once you finish this, you might want to read the most widely read speech of all time – *The Sermon on the Mount.*

Leaders' speeches are not the only place to find the dynamics of the PAR leadership skills. Want to see PAR in action? Just read the recollections of Allied Signal's former CEO Larry Bossidy in his book, *Execution: The Discipline of Getting Things Done,* or former General Electric CEO Jack Welch's bestseller, *Straight from the Gut. My American Journey* by former U.S. Secretary of State and U.S. General Colin Powell and former Secretary of State George Schultz's *Turmoil and Triumph* are also filled with PAR skills as are countless other memoirs of other successful leaders in both the public and private sectors.

To see the absence of these leadership skills, you only need to look at the ashes of Enron, WorldCom, and other recognized business and personal failures.

About now, you are probably thinking that the Decision Ladder and PAR obviously work for these recognized leaders, but the likelihood of your becoming Secretary of State, or leading a Fortune 100 company, or inspiring a nation is probably slim. So, the question now becomes, how do you make PAR work for **you**?

During our PAR training sessions, participants are asked to deliver a short, inspiring presentation to the group. Initially, most people seem to dread this assignment, but in the end, they actually end up loving the exercise.

The instructions for the presentation are relatively simple: First, the participants must select a topic and recommendation about which they are passionate, knowledgeable, and willing to share with an audience.

Then, they must give a three- to five-minute presentation designed to inspire the audience to become increasingly involved and ultimately become committed to the topic.

The presentation should accomplish three objectives:

Open with a Decision Goal that includes a call to action.

Align with each level on the Decision Ladder in order from bottom to top.

End with tangible proof (a show of hands, giving money, signing up, taking action, etc.) that the audience is committed to the idea.

Giving such a presentation, one that follows the Decision Ladder, helps our PAR training participants fully think through their ideas and practice **RAISING** in a way that makes it easy for others to follow.

During one of our training sessions with a client that was attempting to increase its customer-service competency, the participants were asked to do this presentation exercise. This time, however, some of the participants asked the *Cracking the Code* author who was directing the session to give an example of a Decision Ladder presentation.

The following speech is the one the author delivered, as he tied in both the objective of the session and the objective of the presentation exercise.

*"The responsibility of each and every one of us is to let businesses know how they are doing at meeting our expectations. In a world where our economy is global, doing so is in all of our best interests. I would like to share an idea of how you can help do this, and you can decide if you wish to participate. (**DECISION GOAL**)*

*"Does anyone really care? It seems that most businesses neglect their customers today. Across the board, customer service is just not what it used to be, and it appears to be getting worse as time goes by. If we fail to take any action, we are in fact saying that we are satisfied with the service we get, and the result is that everyone's expectations are lowered. (**NEGLECT**)*

*"Because so many of us believe that we just do not have the time to get involved in critiquing the service we are receiving, we make statements such as, 'I just want to eat and leave' or 'I have to get to the airport.' There just are simply too many other demands taking up our time. (**COMPLAIN**)*

*"Who wants to get involved? The act of confronting poor service, which is uncomfortable for most people, is something we would rather avoid. This type of confrontation can cause anxiety to develop and even make some people physically sick. (**AVOID**)*

*"How often have you heard someone say, 'It's not our job!' or 'I just won't go back there again!' If businesses deliver bad service, it will not be long before they are out of business. In fact, I have been waiting for several companies to do just that, but to my surprise, they keep hanging on. Unfortunately, the result is that service has hit lows everywhere. So, where are we going to go? (**STOP**)*

*"Does it really make a difference? Can one person make that big of a difference? Who is going to make the effort to change anything based on one critique? (**CHALLENGE**)*

"These are excuses all of us have used at one time or another to mind our own business and go our own way. All I ask of you is to give me just a few minutes of your time to consider an approach and its potential, and in the end, you decide whether to take part. (**LOOK/LISTEN**)

"Just this morning I found this feedback card on the table in my hotel room. The card was promptly displayed in a holder with several other cards in place. I imagine someone in this hotel chain must care about this feedback card. Notice the card is in color and well designed to attract attention. (**STUDY**)

"Someone probably went to great lengths to design this card. It has little boxes to check, so I do not have to write anything out. It does not seem like it would take me long at all to fill the card out. Less than a minute I would imagine. (**STUDY**)

"I am not even required to put my name on it. That is completely up to me. I have the option to leave the card in the room or drop it off in the box on the way out of the hotel. MMMmm. No confrontation necessary. That is a relief. (**STUDY**)

"Letting people know how they are doing is important, and I am not just talking about poor performance either. What if they perform really well? We should let them know that too! (**CONTINUE**)

"Let me tell you what you can get by letting others know how they are doing. I have received free meals, a night's stay, and gift cards sent to me for just taking the action of telling businesses how they are doing at customer satisfaction. I can tell you from my experience, someone does care. Some of you undoubtedly have a story of what you were given when you commented on someone's customer service. (**PLAY** WITH THE FOLLOWING STORY.)

"Here is a true customer-service story that happened to my wife and me. One year my wife and I attended practice day at the renowned Masters Golf Tournament at the Augusta National Golf Club in Augusta, Georgia.

186

"Our day at this cathedral of golf was amazing. The grass was like carpet; flowers were in bloom everywhere; and the course was filled with golf superstars.

"We saw Jumbo Osaki make a Hole-in-One on 16 and Arnold Palmer enthusiastically hug and kiss a woman fan. We even followed Greg Norman for awhile, but nothing beat the thrill we had as we trailed legendary Jack Nicklaus for several holes.

"We were among some 75,000 people that day at the practice round, and my wife couldn't wait to tell her dad about our experience. She wanted him to visit us the next year so that he could go to Augusta with us and experience a practice round at the Masters.

"Unfortunately, tournament officials closed the practice round to the general public for the next year. Because of the high turnout when we were there and because attendance for the actual tournament is usually around 25,000, the officials decided to create an attendance lottery for the practice round.

"My wife was upset, extremely upset. Now, until she met me, my wife would never have taken time to tell anyone how she felt regarding customer service. She was definitely nonconfrontational. Of course, instead of letting a business know about its poor service, she would bend my ear in the car all the way home, talking about the poor service she received.

"This time though, she wrote a letter to the Masters Tournament chairman, letting him know of her disappointment. She told him how her day at the practice round was one of the best days she has ever had and that she was so upset that she could not share the experience with her dad.

"Now, the Augusta National Golf Club is legendary for not responding to criticism in any manner. To my surprise, the chairman responded, sending my wife a letter to explain the reasons for closing the practice day to the general public. He even thanked her and expressed his gratitude that she had a wonderful day at Augusta National.

"That alone would have been proof positive to me that businesses appreciate our feedback. But there was more...Augusta National later sent my wife four tickets for the next Masters' practice day. (ULTIMATE **PLAY***)*

*"So, you see, sharing your opinions about customer service is appreciated. That said, I thank you for your time, and now I am going to return to my seat, complete this comment card, and let this hotel know how well they have done these past few days." (***COMMIT***)*

After delivering his speech, our speaker returned to his seat and next to him was a stack of hotel critique cards. As he started to answer his, he soon heard participants around the room ask, "Could I have one of those cards to fill out too?"

The speech inspired others to act. The speaker got followers. He inspired others to commit. So, he got a big win. What happened is called leadership, and you can do the same.

Another *Cracking the Code* author, an outspoken advocate for motorcycle safety, experienced the death of his 25-year-old son in a motorcycle accident more than a dozen years ago. Since then, this author has distributed hundreds and hundreds of the purple-and-white bumper stickers that promote motorcycle safety, by delivering presentations, such as the one below, and moving his audience up the Decision Ladder.

"The current level of carnage on the highways throughout the United States has reached intolerable levels. I am convinced that each of us has a responsibility to do our part in stemming the ever-increasing death rate. Today, I would like to share with you a simple safety campaign that you can participate in, and at the end of my presentation, you can decide whether or not you wish to be involved. **(DECISION GOAL)** You can signify your willingness to be involved just by raising your hand. **(PROOF OF COMMITMENT)**

"When you travel, I know each of you have seen enough idiotic driving so that you cannot be indifferent to the idea of making our streets safer. **(NEGLECT)**

"Let me share with you some troubling national statistics. Each year, the total number of traffic deaths in the United States hovers around 20,000 people with more than 1,000,000 serious injuries. All you need to do is pick up a local newspaper to read about the latest traffic accident victims. **(COMPLAIN)**

"The really scary part of these statistics is that we are killing ten times as many people in traffic accidents in a single year as America lost in military casualties during four years of the Iraq war. **(AVOID)**

"The increasing American losses in Iraq caused many in the United States to rise up and demand an end to that conflict. I think Americans must also rise up and demand an end to the horrendous death rate on our nation's highways. **(STOP)**

"The real challenge for most of us is that the highway death problem is so immense and so complex that we find it hard to believe we can have an impact. And, if we were to tackle the whole problem, it is probably insurmountable. **(CHALLENGE)**

"What I am suggesting is a simple safety campaign that involves one small segment of highway travelers. It involves you merely placing this bumper sticker on your personal vehicle. Let me explain. (**LOOK/LISTEN**)

LOOK TWICE - SAVE A LIFE
MOTORCYCLES ARE EVERYWHERE

"In one year alone, over 4,000 motorcyclists were killed and over 100,000 more seriously injured in motorcycle highway accidents. Approximately 75% of those accidents involved a motorcycle colliding with a car or a truck. The fatality rate for motorcyclists is almost four times higher than for occupants of passenger cars, and per mile driven, a motorcyclist is 35 times more likely to die in a crash than an automobile passenger. (**STUDY**)

"Let me give you a couple of interesting facts regarding motorcycle accidents:

"1. In the vast majority of collisions involving a motorcycle and car/truck, the driver of the car/truck usually says, 'I never saw the motorcycle.' And you know what; those drivers probably did not because when most of us are driving, we are not looking for motorcycles. The issue then is education, not negligence.

"2. Over 25 years ago, a mother started a campaign to reduce deaths due to drunk driving. And although we still have a long way to go, Mothers Against Drunk Driving (MADD) has made considerable progress in its safety campaigns, cutting deaths by drunk driving almost in half since 1980. Yes, it is possible for one person to make a difference. (**CONTINUE**)

"For a moment, just imagine the impact you can have with this purple-and-white bumper sticker. Assume that in your daily travels you encounter 100 other cars. Even though in most U.S. urban centers, this number is considerably higher, but let us be conservative. That means by placing this bumper sticker on your personal vehicle for one year, you will make 36,500 impressions.

"Now, imagine that one driver out of the 36,500 does LOOK TWICE, and that one look prevents a potential motorcycle fatality.

"What if that motorcyclist turns out to be the future research scientist who discovers a cure for cancer, or the agronomist who solves world hunger, or the economist who solves world poverty? Or perhaps the motorcyclist is your son or daughter? **(PLAY)**

"To date, more than a half million of these stickers have been distributed throughout the world. The Look Twice – Save A Life *slogan has appeared on billboards, bus stop benches, and taxicab toppers throughout the United States. I am convinced that this campaign has saved lives, and I would like to see a show of hands of those who are willing to join this campaign by placing this bumper sticker on your personal vehicle. Thank you."* **(COMMIT)**

So, like our fellow author, do you have a passion that would be better served if you could influence more people to become involved? This presentation and its incorporation of the Decision Ladder, at the very least, should provide a template for you to use as you pursue your passion and work to improve your part of the world.

While you might never have the opportunity to inspire a group of people to take on a cause about which you are passionate, the methodology of using the Decision Ladder to prepare a speech is an excellent tool for preparing for a meeting or simple conversation to reach a decision.

Here is an exercise to help you use the Decision Ladder in various presentation scenarios. Consider that you have an idea that you would like to promote to your manager or an executive within your organization. Now, take at least two or three positions at each level on the Decision Ladder.

NEGLECT

What part of your idea would your manager or executive be indifferent to and how would they express their **NEGLECT**? How would you acknowledge that point of view and discover what is important to them?

COMPLAIN

What difficulty would your idea cause the organization or them personally, and how would they express that complaint? How would you acknowledge **COMPLAIN** and what could you do to resolve that problem?

AVOID

What are the potential personal or organizational risks associated with your idea, and how would your manager or executive express **AVOID**? How would you acknowledge that point of view and create an action plan that either eliminates or minimizes that risk?

STOP

What personal or business reasons could present opposition to your plan, and how would **STOP** sound? How could you acknowledge that point of view and what questions would you ask to fully understand the opposition?

CHALLENGE

What skepticism could your manager or executive express or what potential challenges does your idea cause, and what would those **CHALLENGES** sound like? How would you acknowledge that some proof is needed, and are you prepared to deal with those potential challenges?

(You will see CHALLENGE more than any other attitude when you attempt to sell your idea up an organization. Most business executives use CHALLENGE as a time management tool and challenge most new ideas, knowing full well that the vast majority are not fully developed and need more work. Those they effectively send back for more development. However, if you are prepared for the initial challenge, most executives will give you time today. A word to the wise.)

LOOK/LISTEN

Consider all the information that your manager or executive would want or need to "know" to arrive at a conclusion. How would you acknowledge that openness and launch into your plan?

STUDY

What details would they need to analyze in order to reach a decision? How would you acknowledge that need to consider the facts or need to "know" and either help them STUDY or give them the time to think it through?

CONTINUE

What are the advantages of your idea? How would your idea be better for the company and themselves? What other questions will your manager or executive likely have? Are you ready with the appropriate answers?

PLAY

Picture the benefits that would be important to your manager or executive. What result would be good for both the company and them? Help them see the possibilities.

COMMIT

What action is the appropriate next step to move your plan forward? How will you draw the conversation to conclusion? What is the optimum outcome for this conversation? What is the minimum expectation?

Understand that in this exercise, you most likely will never hit the exact words that your manager or executive will use in each situation. However, what you will do is prepare yourself for every possible reaction on the Decision Ladder. This preparation will give you more confidence, so that ultimately your manager or executive is buying the confidence you show in your idea and buying the business soundness of your idea. This exercise should help you prepare on both fronts.

Now you know how corporate and national leaders engage their followers. Additionally, you have a template for delivering an inspiring presentation. And finally, you have a simple exercise to help you prepare for those milestones in your career that become the cornerstones of your success.

The question is no longer IF you are capable of leadership and influencing others. The issue is WHEN. When are you going to step out and try influencing others to follow you? Knowing WHEN is why the subsequent chapter on performance measurement is the next key component in your leadership development.

Chapter 11

Measuring Your Performance

The difference between professionals and amateurs is that amateurs practice until they can get it right, and professionals practice until they cannot get it wrong. We want you to practice like a professional. Practice your PAR skills until they become natural, like muscle memory, and, in turn, you cannot get them wrong.

At this point, you have *cracked* the code to the skills of leadership, and if you were in our training sessions, you would practice your newfound skills with our coaching you to a level of conscious competence. You would, as do those who take part in our PAR training programs, be able to build the feel for using the PAR skills in the context of your business, your issues, your various roles in life, and your responsibilities.

Unfortunately, this hands-on, professional coaching is not available through a book. But you can practice your skills using the exercises sprinkled throughout our book, and then evaluate your performance using the coaching tools you will find in this chapter. To help coach you, we have included:

A simple method for appraising how well your personal influencing skills affect tangible work results,

A way to measure your return on investment, and

A way to assess leadership and teamwork at any level in your organization.

First, we want you to start with this simple action assignment. On a blank sheet of paper, write your answers to these three questions:

If you knew that you absolutely could not fail, what is the greatest professional goal you can imagine committing the rest of your career towards achieving?

How would you describe, in some detail, what it would be like to have successfully arrived at that goal?

What indicators or proof would you want on a daily basis that would indicate progress towards that goal?

Keep your answers closeby as you work through this chapter.

Performance Tracking

All well-run businesses track performance, so they can understand what is working and what is not working compared to their goals and strategies. Every business uses financial indicators. Most businesses use other performance measures, i.e. productivity, safety, market share, customer service, and a variety of other nonfinancial tools to gauge performance. Measuring performance is the management process or the control system for business, and it works.

You should have performance measurements as part of your annual performance appraisal because that appraisal directly impacts your income. Performance is your responsibility. Managers may help, give feedback, and coach but, ultimately, responsibility lies with you. If this is true, then why aren't more employees assuming responsibility for their performance and actions as businesses do?

When we ask people why they have not taken the responsibility yet, we hear a variety of different reasons or excuses, with people telling us:

"I'm too busy."

"I don't know how."

"I don't see the value in it at my level."

"It takes too much time or effort."

"It is my boss's job."

"I don't like the paperwork."

"My job cannot be measured."

"It's not required."

"My annual raise is my measure."

Taking responsibility is not that difficult, and we believe that most people would do so if they had a common-sense, simple, does-not-take-much-time tracking system that they knew how to use and that had immediate personal value.

We created such a tracking system for you to use. Our really simple system measures only two aspects of performance: Activities and Results.

The Key Indicators – Activities and Results

The key indicators of leadership begin with the high payoff activities that contribute to success on a regular basis. Think about what those high payoff activities are for you. To start performance tracking, simply count the number of times you engage in those activities. Fortunately, these activities are easy to define and quantify. After you see how the data can be obtained and analyzed, you will be in a sound position to make better self-management and leadership decisions on a regular basis.

Start by recording your number of attempts each day. An attempt is defined as any decision-seeking interaction you make with other people face-to-face or over the phone. Email attempts only count if you have nothing else to measure.

Then, record the number of decisions you receive when making those attempts. A decision is a **YES** or **NO** response about followership, commitment, and/or cooperation. **YES** and **NO** to all or part of your idea are the only recordable decisions at this point. A **MAYBE** does not count. This will require a lot of discipline from you, but this is absolutely essential for evaluation. (Recording a **MAYBE** as a decision will hurt your performance appraisal later.)

Of course, the purpose of making attempts and getting decisions is to achieve more *customers,* more **YES** responses, and more productive work results. Tracking results is valuable, but just at this point only track decisions – **YES** or **NO**. With this exercise, we want you to focus solely on the number of times you attempt leadership and the number of times those attempts end in getting committed decisions.

Besides increasing your productivity immediately, this activity strongly reinforces your use and effectiveness of the PAR skill set. This is how the process works: Starting today, keep a personal record of all the ATTEMPTS you make in seeking followers, buy-in or customers. Also, record whether you got a DECISION at the end of each conversation.

You may get some **MAYBES**, and your ATTEMPTS and DECISIONS probably will not be equal. The object is to just keep trying, and you will become more focused, more results oriented, and much more likely to use these leadership skills in every situation.

At the end of each workday, take the time to post your number of ATTEMPTS and DECISIONS onto a piece of graph paper. Do this for 21 consecutive workdays, and watch as a trend line starts to develop. *(Two sample graphs can be found later in this chapter.)*

Remember that a *MAYBE* is a time waster. When you have a *MAYBE*, ask yourself if that *MAYBE* is from someone who is really at **STUDY** or is that person just avoiding telling you *NO*? Or is the **AVOID** a stall or indecision? Using a *MAYBE* instead of a **NO** is fairly commonplace. *"Go ask your mother"* or *"Just send me some information, and I will get back to you"* are two perfect examples.

One of our PAR participants, Alan Smada, told us that he recognized this happening to him. "I got so sick of getting *MAYBEs* that I started listing them as **NOs** on my graph because they were 'No, for now.' As soon as I started acknowledging MAYBEs as **NOs**, my percentage of **YESs** went up."

To show you how to track your ATTEMPTS and DECISIONS over the 21-day period, we have included two sample graphs. On the graphs, we used an A to symbolize ATTEMPTS and a D for DECISIONS, and we recommend that you do the same to keep your chart simple and readable at a quick glance.

Example 1 shows how the distance between ATTEMPTS and DECISIONS narrows over time, with fewer *MAYBES* and greater leadership.

Sample Attempt and Decision Graphs

Example #1

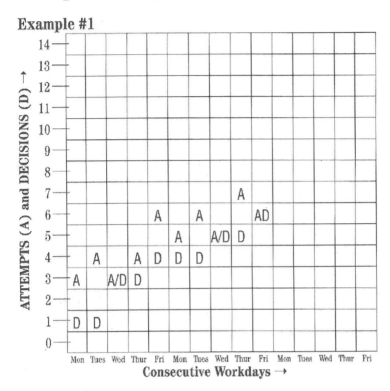

This graph shows:

1st	Mon:	Had 3 Attempts, 1 Decision
	Tues:	Had 4 Attempts, 1 Decision
	Wed:	Had 3 Attempts, 3 Decisions
	Thur:	Had 4 Attempts, 3 Decisions
	Fri:	Had 6 Attempts, 4 Decisions
2nd	Mon:	Had 5 Attempts, 4 Decisions
	Tues:	Had 6 Attempts, 4 Decisions
	Etc.	

The gap between ATTEMPTS and DECISIONS is small and gets smaller over time, indicating fewer "Maybes." Overall leadership activity trend is increasing, probably heading towards increased productivity and results.

The second example is not as positive as the first. In this chart, you can see a downward trend, which could indicate a problem. The DECISION rate is dropping and so is the number of ATTEMPTS made.

Sample Attempt and Decision Graphs

Example #2

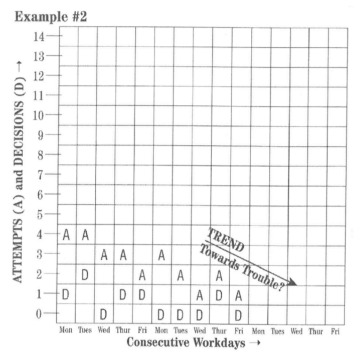

This second ATTEMPTS and DECISIONS graph shows:

1st	Mon:	Had 4 Attempts, 1 Decision
	Tues:	Had 4 Attempts, 2 Decisions
	Wed:	Had 3 Attempts, 0 Decisions
	Thur:	Had 3 Attempts, 1 Decision
	Fri:	Had 2 Attempts, 1 Decision
2nd	Mon:	Had 3 Attempts, 0 Decisions
	Tues:	Had 2 Attempts, 0 Decisions
	Etc.	

This graph shows low decision closure rate and decreasing activity. May be heading for trouble. Possibly working hard, but with few leadership actions. Probably not communicating very much.

Analyzing Trends

After you record your 21 workdays of ATTEMPTS and DECISIONS, we want you to do your own trend analysis. To do that, study your graphs and ask yourself:

Is the gap between ATTEMPTS and DECISIONS too wide for your satisfaction?

Is your trend line decreasing? If so, why?

Is your trend line increasing? If so, what did you learn from your success?

What is the correlation between ATTEMPTS and DECISIONS? Bottom-line results? Did you get more accomplished? What was morale like? Yours? Others?

Which skills improved the most? What worked well?

What did not work well? What can you do about it?

If your trend line decreased or your work results are less than satisfactory, you may have some investigating to do. However, lack of results does not mean failure. If that were true, then every company that has a bad quarter would quit and dissolve. Companies do not quit. They investigate and problem solve. They make changes. You can do that also.

If your trend analysis or results are disappointing or not at the level you want, consider these tough questions:

Is your job knowledge adequate?

Are you well prepared for meetings?

Are you working at capacity?

Are you focused on the right things?

What is your goal?

What is your motivation level? (Remember you cannot lead anyone any higher than your own level on the Decision Ladder.)

Are you looking for decisions or are you pushing for a YES only response?

Are you triangulating negative points of view?

Are you using your PAR skills?

You should be ready now to analyze your own performance. To help you do just that, we prepared a Problem Solving Reference Chart designed as a starting point for you in determining your improvement sources and/or actions. We outlined various situations along with possible improvement sources or actions for you to implement.

Problem-Solving Reference Chart

The Keys to Self-Managed Success at Leadership

The columns below illustrate the 24 situations possible when you analyze your Performance Tracking graph of ATTEMPTS, DECISIONS and RESULTS (Key Indicators of Your Goal). Use this information as a point of reference to begin analyzing, investigating and solving the problems of achieving your objectives.

SITUATION			IMPROVEMENT SOURCES/ACTIONS
ATTEMPTS Graph Trend	**DECISIONS** Graph Trend	**RESULTS** Key Indicators	**Starting Point for Deciding**
Many	Many	OK	• Do more of the same activities. Do not change your work habits. What you're doing is working. • Focus on efficiency. You are doing right things; see if you can do them faster.
Many	Many	Not OK	• Check validity of ATTEMPTS and DECISIONS. • Check basic assumptions about your approach. • Check probing, aligning, raising and closure skills.
Few	Many	OK	• Talking to enough people? More possible? • Counting all the ATTEMPTS? • If yes to above questions, then no problem.
Few	Many	Not OK	• Check validity of the data. • Go for bigger decisions. • Talking to the right Deciders? • Getting maybe's but calling them decisions?
Many	Few	OK	• Relying on too few sources? • Asking for back-up decisions? • Going for all or nothing?
Many	Few	Not OK	• Check all "PAR" skills level. • Is your motivation level the problem? • Are there questions/resistance you can't answer? • Need more knowledge?
Few	Few	OK	• Relying on too few sources? • Risking as much as possible?
Few	Few	Not OK	• Check your work habits. • Check your goals. Have they changed? • Check your motivation level. • Check your procedural or technical knowledge. • Make more ATTEMPTS—immediately. • Back to basics or out of business.

The columns on the chart illustrate the 24 situations possible when you analyze your Performance Tracking graph of ATTEMPTS, DECISIONS, and RESULTS (which are all key indicators of your goal). Use this information as a point of reference to begin analyzing, investigating, and solving the problems of achieving your objectives.

Performance Measurement

By participating in the Performance Tracking activity and using the Problem Solving Reference Chart, you are appraising your own performance on a daily basis. Admittedly, you are only analyzing your leadership skills and looking at your key indicators and results. But all the elements of what-to-do and how-to-go-about performance appraisal are contained in that process, a process that is highly objective.

If you are an individual contributor, you can apply the same process to your most important project and responsibility. You even can use this data with your manager during your next formal performance appraisal. Doing so is a real confidence builder. Better still, keep your manager informed about what you are doing and what is happening as it happens. You might even get some welcome assistance, good ideas, and greater credibility.

If you are a team leader, you can apply this same measurement process to your team when everyone is working toward a common goal. Combine the individual data of your team members into a huge team graph. As you try this team measurement, we are confident that you will find the process breeds teamwork like you have never seen before.

When you track performance activity for your team, keep these points in mind:

Maintain the graph current daily and make sure it is visible to the entire team.

Acknowledge individuals for every single contribution to the overall graph results.

Make certain that your team's results can be counted in numbers and are not abstractions.

Celebrate as soon as your team meets a target goal. Then start over with new, different, or higher goals.

Celebrate fantastically when your team achieves fantastic success. Get publicity for your team. Take pictures. Arrange interviews.

Congratulate yourself.

How can you tell when leadership and teamwork occur? Sometimes *general impressions* may be enough of an indicator. However, having specific data to support those impressions is even better. If you are going to appraise your own and others' leadership abilities, you must accurately appraise both your performance and their performance.

Leadership and teamwork can be measured in terms of successful actions and results. In the next chapter, we share even more applications and ways to lead and work with teams.

Conclusion

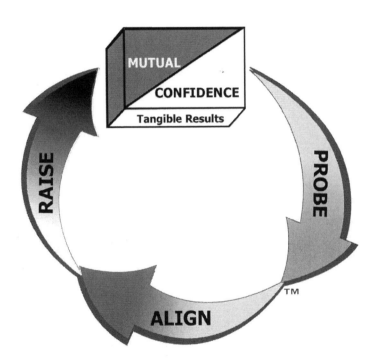

Chapter 12

Leadership: Your Sustainable Competitive Advantage

An organization's ability to learn, and translate that learning into action rapidly, is the ultimate competitive advantage.

Jack Welch

There is a big difference between making a quality product and obtaining a quality performance from someone. A product is something that is engineered, measured, manipulated, and easily changed to fit any set of specifications. To make a quality product out of raw materials, you need a tool set that includes mathematics, physics, and statistical measurements.

People, on the other hand, are another story. Unlike products, people cannot be engineered, measured, manipulated, or easily changed to fit any set of specifications. To obtain a quality performance, you need a far different set of tools than you would use to make a product.

The key to a quality performance and to influencing another person and gaining that person's cooperation and commitment to a job well done can be summed up in one word: Willingness. And as an effective leader, you must address the issues involved in willingness. So, in this chapter, we focus on how you can use your leadership as a tool, not only to encourage willingness and gain commitment from employees, but also to:

Help employees work within the rules, and

Enhance average performance.

We will also show you how to apply leadership skills to sales and customer service and ultimately how you can:

Turn prospective customers into committed customers, and

Provide customers with superior customer service experiences.

Lastly, we will touch on some of the limitations that New Media places on leadership and your ability to communicate with others and gain their wholehearted support and commitment for a common course of action.

Leadership for Living within the Rules

Sometimes poor results at work trace back to a simple problem of someone not following work rules. Do not view an employee's not following the rules as a performance problem, because true performance issues center on quality or quantity of work. Living within the rules is a separate issue that only refers to accepting company policies and procedures. It is important that you recognize this difference because when you manage or lead others, this is an issue you probably will have to handle at some time.

How often have you wanted to say "Just do it!" as a quick solution to getting an employee to accept a company rule or policy? While this may give you the results you want, this is an ineffective way to gain someone's acceptance of company rules. As you know, some rules and policies are important in every successful enterprise.

A difficult, but necessary, job of any team leader or manager is gaining acceptance of acknowledged work rules. Living within the rules can occasionally be a problem for an employee. Often, you will find that your best performer is the one who wants to bend the rules a bit. While some rules can be stretched, others, such as safety rules, hours of work, product specifications, etc., are inflexible and must be followed.

Although bending the rules may not affect the performance of your better employees, that may not be the case for others in your work group. Allowing some to bend or not follow the rules can lead to perceived unfairness and problems with other members of the group.

To help you help your employees comply with work rules, we have outlined six distinct action steps. By coupling these steps with your leadership skills, you can gain and maintain your employees' commitment to company rules and policies.

Action Steps

Describe the correct behavior needed that would be in accord with the work rules. (Focus specifically on the solution. If you do not critique the error or the problem, your entire conversation could end successfully right away. Also, speak from very high on the Decision Ladder. If you sound below Neutral, you invite defensiveness.)

Explain why that desired behavior is needed. (Describe the impact of the employee's current behavior on the work or the work group. Triangulate negative and/or defensive reactions, i.e. make the problem an 'IT'. Respect Acknowledgements throughout will keep the conversation alive.)

Investigate why the problem exists. (Use Rapport Acknowledgements and as many NIQCL questions as you need to obtain a complete mutual understanding of the situation.)

Restate the work rule and ask what can be done to change behavior. (Check understanding of the rule or rules, acknowledge, and then ask for suggestions before offering your own ideas. Align for teamwork.)

Discuss the suggestions and find the best solution. (Lead the conversation to Neutral and higher up the Decision Ladder for a quality result.)

Seek a commitment. (**COMMIT** to action. Invest the few extra minutes needed to get a total quality outcome. Commitments yield quality. Agreements, good intentions at that moment in time, are both easily broken and often resented.)

To prepare for those employee conversations about following rules, try these three valuable tips:

Determine the ideal outcome for your conversation.

Define the minimum acceptable outcome for the conversation. (Any decision within these parameters is a win.)

Anticipate all potential problems beforehand. (Determine how you would acknowledge and align with each issue. Doing this in advance can be a great confidence builder for you.)

Leadership for Enhancing Average Performance

Managerial and team leaders always strive for superior performance wherever and whenever possible. Unfortunately, if too many on a team barely meet acceptable standards, that team likely will miss its goals. The most overlooked resource for increasing work quality and quantity is the average performer. When you are in the role of manager or team leader, you need to recognize this and keep in mind that your average performers will be the key to your group successfully meeting its goals.

Paying attention to performance extremes is all too easy. Top producers have built-in rewards, and because their performance top the charts, it is easy to give them meaningful and specific feedback. Since they depend on their top performers, most managers and team leaders let those performers know how much they are valued.

Performance at the opposite end of the spectrum also gets attention. Below target performance is visible to everyone involved in the effort, which means managers and team leaders have no choice but to try to make improvements.

This day-to-day pressure of working with underachievers often results in the manager or leader neglecting or overlooking the average performers. As a result, an average performance can easily erode and turn into a performance problem.

The upside is that as a leader, you have the ability to influence an average performance to a higher level. By identifying and strongly acknowledging specific aspects of your employees' performance that are above standard, you can reinforce their confidence in their abilities to perform better than average in other areas as well.

However, when you address these areas of opportunity, be careful to maintain your employees' self-esteem and not to imply a performance deficiency. The idea is to make good performers better, to build strength-on-strength, and not to give the impression of a *problem.* The following five steps and your leadership skills will help you do just that.

Action Steps

Describe an aspect of the person's performance that is above standard and explain why it deserves special recognition. (Be specific about the person's successes. Show positive emotion. Connect that back to the objectives of your group/department/division/company.)

Express appreciation and desire to help in other aspects of performance. (Show high INTEREST to **PLAY** in helping develop other capabilities as well.)

Suggest another area where the person might excel. (Use a Decision Goal, such as "I believe you could also excel in the area of _____. Let's discuss that so you can decide whether or not that is doable.")

Discuss the action steps needed to produce this higher level of performance. (Lead to NEUTRAL and above. Ask for the person's suggestions first. **PLAY** with different approaches before closing at the biggest **COMMITMENT** the individual can make today. Remember the Decision Goal.)

Summarize and express your confidence in the person. (Summarize next steps, what support you will provide, and your confidence.)

However, before you have that discussion with that employee about performance, you need to consider two things: *the ideal outcome of your conversation, and the minimum acceptable outcome for that conversation.* Any decision in between those parameters is a win, and the ideal outcome is a BIG win.

Leadership for Sales Professionals

If you are a sales professional and have read this far, you have already discovered innumerable ways the PAR leadership skills can help you reach the aggressive sales targets you set for yourself.

From our years of working with sales professionals, we know that achieving those aggressive goals is challenging enough for you, especially since there are so many sales amateurs are out there making your job all the more difficult. Decision makers across all industries are growing increasingly frustrated, as they waste their time with these amateurs, salespeople who are ill prepared for true business discussions.

Deciders are being inundated with salespeople promoting products and services without ever connecting to the Deciders' needs and/or wants. As a consequence, increasing numbers of Deciders are both insulating themselves from all salespeople and adding another barrier to the efficiency of the sales process.

True sales professionals, however, see this as just another opportunity to create a sustainable competitive advantage and a way to move out of the vendor ranks and into the stratified air of Trusted Advisor.

You can make that transition to Trusted Advisor by simply starting every business conversation with a solid Decision Goal. Let us review the Decision Goal as it relates to sales, and then you can determine whether or not using Decision Goals will separate you from the also-rans.

In Chapter 3, we introduced the three criteria of good Decision Goals, pointing out that effective leaders:

Show they are **Confident** in the goals they advocate,

Invite Others to Neutral as they explain the strategy for achieving the goals, and

Acknowledge others (their followers) as **Decision** makers.

In a sales application, when you make that initial confident statement, you demonstrate that you are knowledgeable about the product/service you represent, are skillful in your ability to influence others, and have an intimate understanding of the value or benefit your product/service brings to the customer.

Working on sales force development with clients across a wide variety of industries, we find that most of our clients do a reasonably good job of educating their sales personnel on the ins and outs of their product lines and/or service capabilities.

Yet, even though their sales forces have strong product knowledge, these same clients recognize a deficiency in their sales personnel's ability to influence. That is why they bring us in to work with the sales teams to enhance their existing skill levels. Because of our successful track record and the exclusive guarantee [i] we offer, our clients are reasonably assured, as a result of our engagement, that they will get the desired skill level they want from their sales team.

The secret for making that transition is having an intimate understanding of the value or benefit that your product/service brings to your prospective customer. Without that, you will be grouped with the amateurs. So, how do you obtain this information?

Because a good deal of this information is a matter of public record, you can find most of what you need through the popular Internet search engines, business publications, or business intelligence firms. Other sales professionals, trade associations, the Chamber of Commerce, and additional business organizations also can offer additional background information.

However, information from these sources is usually not enough to give you the confidence you need to engage in a reasonable business discussion with a prospect.

Ultimately, the critical information can only come from the Decision Makers themselves. And with a good, solid Decision Goal, you should be able to obtain the information you need from the Decision Maker and determine if your product/service is of value to that Decision Maker.

Let's take a look at how using a Decision Goal would work in an initial conversation. For instance, when we at PAR make an initial call to a prospective client, the conversation sounds something like this:

> *"Hello, this is John Smith from The PAR Group. I'm calling because we have helped a number of companies similar to yours with their sales force development. While I have done a good deal of preliminary research on your organization, I don't have enough specific information to state with any certainty that The PAR Group can help you also. I'd like to talk briefly with you to find out more about your goals and specific needs, so we can determine if a more in-depth discussion is appropriate."*

This type of initial approach reveals an extensive amount of information which permits actual Decision Goals that start real business discussions and achieves that sustainable competitive advantage of Trusted Advisor.

The following opening call scenarios effectively show how Decision Goals can work in a variety of different industries.

An Animal Health Client

"We believe that customer compliance is one of the biggest challenges facing most veterinarians. I'd like to show you a few of (company name) innovations that are solving that challenge. Then you can determine if these should be part of your practice's formulary."

A Food Ingredient Company

"Because of the past scares in the pet food industry, we certainly understand your emphasis on the safety of all the ingredients in your products designed for human consumption. Our quality assurance processes provide the confidence you require. Let me describe our safeguards, so you can decide if (product name) meets and exceeds your standards."

A Financial Services Company

"We believe our electronic trading platform will provide both the cost containment you seek and the security your clients demand. Let me show you how we process option trades, and then you can decide if (company name) should be your preferred electronic platform."

A Technical Services Company

"The reason for my call is that my company has helped many organizations like yours integrate SAP into their applications with less time and disruptions. I would like to talk with you briefly to determine if what we do may be of value to your organization as well."

A Financial/Insurance Service

"I'm calling because we help individuals determine if what they have for retirement and insurance are appropriate to meet their goals. I would like to briefly talk with you to determine if it is worth your time to talk with us in more depth."

A Technical Consulting Company

"There are a number of options to implement the system you have acquired. The one we most recommend is (Option).

Let's discuss why that will give you the best results in a time frame that is right for you, and you decide if that is the right approach for your organization."

Leadership as a Customer Service Skill

Somewhere along the way, some customer service guru, who probably never spent a minute in front of or on the phone with a real customer, determined that there were two golden rules for delivering outstanding customer service. Rule One was *The customer is always right,* and the second rule was something like, *For any other situation, refer to Rule One.*

The service guru's advice sounds good, and perhaps in the magical world of some fable, some business simulation, or some team-bonding experience in the woods, that advice makes perfectly good sense. Unfortunately, real customer service does not take place in fantasyland, in text books, or on rope courses.

Real customer service happens in the real business world between real customers and real frontline employees. In the true world of business, customers react to a lack of information, to limited information, or occasionally even to erroneous information. In real life, rumors many times become facts; suspicions become real; and that coveted prospect becomes the customer from hell. So, perhaps the only refutable law of customer service should be this: *The customer always <u>believes</u> he/she is right.*

Given that this is the reality of business, how can you deliver customer experiences that exceed your customers' expectations every time? The answer lies in two elements of the PAR skills that are absolutely essential to providing superior customer service: 1) Acknowledging a customer's point of view and 2) Aligning solutions to that point of view.

Most customer service failures come when customers do not feel they have been heard or taken seriously. This often occurs when a customer service representative fails to acknowledge the customer's point of view before offering a solution. To prevent this from happening with your customers, you should make Rapport Acknowledgements an essential part of your customer service department.

Sometimes the length of time a customer spends on hold or the number of times a call is transferred makes a situation more difficult. Some of these customers are loud and rude, as they express their disappointments and frustrations. This is all the more reason that your customer service team should acknowledge customers with enough energy to prove to those customers that they are being taken seriously.

Using energy does not mean that your service representative yells back. The energy put into your rep's tone of voice and the emphasis on words spoken should let the customer know that your representative is listening and that the customer matters. If this is a potential issue for your customer service personnel, you may want to review Chapter 4, *Building Rapport*, which deals with acknowledging and listening with empathy.

Secondly, any solution that a customer service rep offers must be aligned with the customer's point of view. For customers at **COMPLAIN,** that means an offer of *Help.*

For customers at **AVOID**, the proper solution would mitigate or eliminate the *Risk.* For customers at **STOP**, the solution would *prevent* future problems. For customers at **CHALLENGE**, the solution would contain the required *proof.* By implementing just these two skills – acknowledging and aligning – within your customer service procedures, you should start exceeding your customers' expectations in no time.

Leadership and the New Media

Change is the only constant. We are not sure who said that, but clearly the author was talking about the way business is conducted. With the advent of the Internet, email, virtual meetings, etc., this New Media has played, and will continue to play, an increasing role in business relationships. At the risk of being labeled Luddites, we must admit that we do not view all these media changes as positive.

Consider the pluses these electronic communication forms offer. They are fast. They are cheap. And they allow you to transfer large bits of information. Today's technology makes people more available than at any time ever before, so that, no matter where you are, you can have access to email, Internet, and phone calls. This is our world today, and who knows what new technology is on the horizon.

However, fast, cheap, and available do not necessarily mean quality. Assume you are trying to close a sale, inspire a member of your team to buy-in to a course of action, obtain funding for your project, or any number of other important business decisions. Which form of New Media would be the most effective to use? Which would work best for critical decision getting? The following graph charts the relationship between cost and quality of each of the major forms of communication now available.

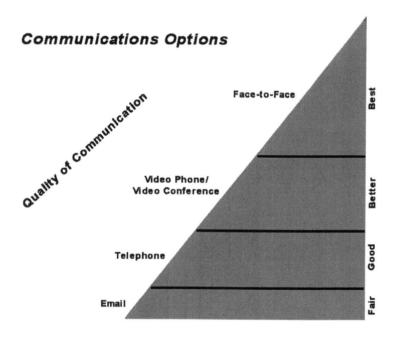

When you look at the different forms of New Media, when compared to the other forms of communications, email, while the least expensive to use, offers the lowest quality of communication for important decisions. With email, the *music* of communication is almost nonexistent. Sure, you can use smiley faces, color changes, and bold type to communicate, but these are poor replacements to you actually hearing people say the words and observing their body language.

A man we know was instant messaging his girlfriend when she took what he had written the wrong way. After jumping in his car and driving across town to explain to her what he really meant in his text message, he decided that instant messaging was not the best approach for some subject matters. His explanation must have worked, as he and his girlfriend are now happily married. However, to this day, he still refuses to instant message his wife.

As in that example, emails can be misunderstood because people do not always read an email with the same emotion or in the same way the writer felt when the message was originally written. Recipients read their emails based on how they feel at that moment in time.

Most everyone is well aware of this, so obviously people know not to use email for major communications such as a performance review. *(Or at least that is what we thought until we read a horror story about a manager who did just that with disastrous results.)* To us, when it comes to important business decisions, email is the worst form of communication.

Next is the telephone call. While more expensive than email, a call does deliver more quality. On a phone call, you can still recognize where someone is on the Decision Ladder. Although with a phone call you hear the words and the person's voice, communication is still limited because you cannot see the person's facial reactions or body language.

When you think about just how well a phone call works to gauge where a person is on the Decision Ladder, think how often, when you are on the phone, that you disguise your real feelings.

Video phones offer even more quality but are substantially more expensive than other New Media. Flat panel-video screens, while they allow you to see other people as they communicate, still cannot project a person's emotions fully. Actors are paid a great deal of money to overact so that their roles appear believable on the video screen.

However, if you stood next to the actors on the set as they gave their video performances, you undoubtedly would say that their actions were greatly exaggerated and larger-than-life. Yet, when watching those same performances on the video screen, you would find the actors quite believable. So, while this medium is better than the phone or email, video communication still fails to capture the true essence of one-on-one communication.

The highest quality of communication is face-to-face. You are able to observe all the *music* of a conversation, and face-to-face gives all involved the opportunity for the most accurate read on the Decision Ladder.

The bigger the impact of a decision, the more likely face-to-face conversation will be the preferred method of communication. For example, when it comes to getting new business, you may use email or mass mail to prospect and call on the phone to qualify the business. But to finalize, you go in person. Or when it comes to hiring a new employee, you may solicit resumes by email and make initial contact via a phone call. Yet, you only hire after a face-to-face interview.

Technology continues to rapidly advance and perhaps some day will advance even to the point of even replacing face-to-face conversation. But until that day happens, face-to-face is still the best way to communicate and the best way to both hear and see the *music* of a conversation.

Chapter 14

Now It Is Up To You

If you were looking for a Chapter 13, you are not going to find one in this book. As embarrassing as it may sound, we are superstitious. So, like the hotel where there is no floor 13, this book goes right from Chapter 12 to Chapter 14 because we do not want to end on 13.

Our society, unfortunately, has come to expect instant gratification. Everyone seems to be looking for the quick fix or the magic pill. This happens all too often in government, business, and everyday life. Important governmental and societal issues that may take years to rectify are reduced to campaign talking points and proposed legislation that only create a whole new set of problems. Unscrupulous executives destroy their companies and end up going to jail because they sacrifice their businesses' long-term viability for short-term results.

Granted these may be extreme examples but consider the everyday consumer who spends hundreds of dollars each year on the latest technology or the latest gadget for instant gratification. Too many individuals also want fast results without putting in the necessary effort. Take dieting for example. Instead of heading to the gym to exercise or cutting back on calories, millions of people search for that magic pill that will make those unwanted pounds melt away.

One of our favorite examples of this quest for instant gratification can be found in the golf industry. Rather than take lessons and spend time at the practice range, so many golfers buy the latest driver to lengthen their drive or compensate for a slice. Golf stores, filled with all sorts of clubs and expensive golf paraphernalia, thrive on those consumers who search for the perfect club or golf tool that will reduce their scores and solve their golfing issues.

Just imagine if golfers spent their money on lessons and buckets of practice balls instead of high-priced clubs. The problem is that lessons and practice are not a quick fix. They require effort and commitment. A golf lesson gives a golfer the necessary skill, and practice hones that skill into proficiency. That, in fact, is the *Magic Pill.*

The same people searching for a magic fix are also the same people who abdicate their personal responsibility. According to one report we heard, 58% of the U.S. workforce has no idea of what is expected of them. That could mean either management has not communicated their expectations, or a large segment of the workforce is so disengaged that they are satisfied just showing up.

These are the workers who create excuses for not achieving better results. In business, you hear these excuses when people say:

"The company didn't..."

"My manager didn't tell me..."

"It's not my fault..."

These are lame excuses used to justify poor performance. There is no commitment. All too many people look for the quick fix instead of working at becoming proficient at an athletic skill, a performing arts skill, or a business skill, like influencing.

Self-examination is extremely difficult, uncomfortable, and something people are hesitant to do. As the lead character in the old cartoon strip *Pogo* once declared, "We have found the problem, and it is us." Obviously, if sticking one's head in the sand worked, then ostriches would rule the world.

So, what does work?

In reality, you cannot change a bad habit. You can only replace it with a better habit that is more likely to give you what you want. Creating a new habit requires willpower that comes from the commitment to put forth the effort.

That is the challenge. Throughout this book, we revealed bit-by-bit the secret to the influencing skills of bona fide leaders. We gave you exercises to practice and test your skills as well as a way to track your skills. We also provided examples of how great leaders intuitively used these skills to achieve massive change. This influencing skill set is the essence of your success whether you are in management, supervision, sales, service, or an executive leadership position.

From our experience, we realize that about 20% of the people who read this book are going to directly tie our PAR skills to their personal and organizational success. Simply by reading this book, this 20% will put those skills into action and have the discipline to practice until they are proficient with each skill.

We also know that another 20% will put this book down after finishing it, say they love the ideas and concepts, place the book on the shelf with their other business improvement books, and then never pick the book up again. These are probably the same quick-fix searching people who have the most technology-advanced golf clubs in their golf bags or the latest no-diet, no-exercise weight-loss products in their medicine cabinets.

Then there are the rest of our readers, the all-important 60% who realize these PAR skills are the key to their personal and professional success but who struggle with acquiring the feel of performing the skills well at will. To these readers, while making perfectly good sense, these skills seem difficult to master.

If you are among this all-important 60 percent, this is where we can help.[6] Our basic business model is to work with companies to customize our training to a company's particular business issues and conduct our in-house training applications at the company's site.

Either we implement the training or we certify the company's internal trainers to implement the applications. We can do this for your company. This way, the PAR Skills become part of your company's corporate culture, so that you can say, as so many of our clients do, *"PAR is the way we do business inside and outside of our organization."*

We help individuals as well. The PAR Group offers quarterly Open Sessions for you if you want hands-on coaching to get the feel of doing the skills well. By participating in these sessions, you take responsibility for your own leadership development.

To find more information on PAR's Open Sessions and the In-House applications we offer, visit our website www.thepargroup.com or call 1-800-247-7188.

When we started writing *Cracking the Code*, our goal was to share what we knew about the secret of leadership so that we could help other people improve their leadership skills and become more effective, capable leaders. We hope that *Cracking the Code* did just that and that the PAR skills will make a difference for you.

Hopefully, you not only enjoyed reading our book, but you also learned some key skills that will help you succeed both at work and in your everyday life. With that said, we wish you continued success.

Authors

G. Thomas Herrington
The PAR Group, Senior Partner

Prior to joining The PAR Group, Senior Partner Tom Herrington spent over ten years in operations, training, and sales management at IBM. During his tenure at IBM, Tom was a National Accounts Marketing representative in Chicago, where he specialized in technology and handled $40 to $50 million projects and contracts for the public sector clients that included the City of Chicago, Chicago Public Schools, and Cook County.

He also worked as the IBM Marketing Manager for the State of Illinois and the IBM Senior Consultant for California and Arizona. Tom's experience at IBM also included work in the company's training and educational group, where he designed and implemented a financial criteria training program.

Part of The PAR Group since 1993, Tom has consulted and presented the PAR program to numerous corporate clients, including such Fortune 500 companies as Honeywell, FirstEnergy, Thomas Cook, IBM, UPS, TLC Laservision, Western-Southern Life Insurance, Sunlife Clarica Insurance, and American Management Systems. In addition to delivering seminars across the United States, he has traveled and consulted with clients on five continents and trained people from an African chieftain to corporate executives to entry-level employees on the PAR skill set. He has delivered multiple PAR sessions in the Netherlands, United Kingdom, France, Sweden, Germany, Mexico, Australia, and New Zealand.

Tom, who has his MBA from the University of Georgia, is a frequent speaker at industry and management conferences, including being a keynote speaker at conferences for the Six Sigma Conference in Atlanta, Georgia, and Thomas Cook in Cancun, Mexico.

Patrick T. Malone
The PAR Group, Senior Partner

Patrick T. Malone, with over thirty-five years of experience in operations and sales management, is a Senior Partner at PAR. Before joining the company in 1989 as Senior Consultant, Patrick worked in a variety of positions from Customer Service to National Sales Manager with the American Greetings Corporation and The Scott Companies.

At The PAR Group, he has worked with a number of Fortune 500 clients, including Hewlett-Packard, Ft. Dodge Animal Health, DuPont, the United Way, Coca-Cola, Delta Air Lines, Siemens Medical, Verizon Wireless, Sensient Technologies, Banfield: The Pet Hospital, and the American Cancer Society. His consultancy has taken him into the global marketplace where he has delivered PAR seminars in Canada, Mexico, the United Kingdom, Spain, Malaysia, Brazil, Australia, China (including Hong Kong), and all over the United States.

Patrick, educated at John Carroll University, is a frequent speaker at industry and management conferences including Frontline Forum of the American School of International Management, the Business Schools at Kennesaw State University and Georgia State University, the Colleges of Veterinary Medicine at Mississippi State, Iowa State, Florida, Minnesota, and Tufts University, and the American Society of Training and Development.

As a member of Sales and Marketing Executives of Atlanta, he held numerous positions in the organization, including Executive Vice President. A member of the Professional Services Executives Roundtable, the CEO Action Group, Patrick has served as the National Board President of The Compassionate Friends, Inc., an international support group for bereaved parents, and is a former Trustee of The TCF Foundation, Inc.

James Georges
The PAR Group, Chief Executive Officer

As the company's Chief Executive Officer, James Georges directs the company's operations on a day-to-day basis. Jim's career at The PAR Group began in 1985, as a part-time employee, working in the company's shipping department while he was still a college student at Mercer University in Atlanta.

After graduating from Mercer with a B.A. degree in broadcast communications, he joined the company fulltime, taking on various roles over the next few years in logistics, customer service, marketing, and inventory management.

Among the many projects that Jim has worked on at PAR has been the production of several PAR training films. Using his background in broadcast communications, he worked as production assistant, producer, and executive producer on PAR productions that won multiple training industry awards, including the prestigious *World Fest Award*, the *Telly Award,* and the *PMN Joey* award.

In 1993, Jim was appointed Chief Financial Officer, and later in 1997, he assumed his current position as CEO. In this role, he has successfully directed The PAR Group's steady, profitable growth.

Jim is also an accomplished still photographer, whose work has been used by nonprofit organizations, printed in annual reports, and posted on various websites.

Endnotes

[1]Lee Iacocca with William Novak, *Iacocca - An Autobiography* (New York: Bantam Books Inc., 1984), 63.

[2] Ibid., 64.

[3] Ibid., 65.

[4] Ibid., 66.

[5] Ibid., 68.

[6] A PAR client receives a 100% return on training material investment within 90 days following the training, or PAR returns that investment upon return of all material.